HOME
LIFE
AROUND
THE
WORLD

ANITA MARTINEZ BEIJER
Author & Photographer

HOME LIFE AROUND THE WORLD

ANITA MARTINEZ BEIJER
Author & Photographer

NEST PUBLISHING

INTRODUCTION

My name is Anita Martinez Beijer and I'm a Swedish interior designer. My work has taken me into countless homes of private customers, as well as into the global market, working for a major Swedish furnishing company. These have been exciting and fruitful years.

But I have felt the need to delve deeper. Beyond the polished surfaces and stylish interiors in the glossy magazines and books that surround us. Behind the curated homes we share on social media. To homes not designed to conform to established trends, but that are truly personal and reflect the people living in them.

During 2015 and 2016 I travelled the world on a quest; what does a home mean? What makes a living space a place we call home? How do we relate to and interact with it? What qualities in our homes do we treasure the most? What dreams and wishes do we have related to our homes?

This quest has taken me to Shanghai, Hong Kong, Cape Town, Buenos Aires, Uruguay, Mexico City and New York. I met an amazing collection of individuals from different walks of life. Architects, designers, photographers and other creatives. Food and art lovers. People passionate about the environment. All with their own stories and destinies.

They not only opened their homes. They also generously shared insightful thoughts and reflections about their homes, as well as their philosophy of life and their personal life stories.

Home life around the world is about the relationship we have with that most private and intimate space – our home.

Anita Martinez Beijer is an author, photographer and interior designer. www.bohemia.life

"It's not coincidental that there is a focus on people and their spaces today. We are so connected, but at the same time we spend so much time actually alone, because so many of our human connections are online. We are presenting carefully chosen images of ourselves on Internet. It makes you wonder, what's behind these digital versions of us?
How do people actually live in real life?"

Emily Johnston

CONTENTS

DOREEN

GARDENS, CAPE TOWN

Doreen de Waal
Business owner
Design consultant
Producer & stylist

AN ACCOMMODATING HOME
GARDENS, CAPE TOWN

"I'm passionate about my family," Doreen tells me. "We are very lucky in that we really like each other and have something to say to one another. Every single member of the family has something to offer in the creative field. It may be different but it's always interesting".

Doreen and her family live in an old, historic house, a former rectory in a leafy, quiet part of Gardens. That is, she shares it with Meyer her husband, their youngest daughter Olivia, who is still at university, and Jinja the dog. Their son Uno lives in Johannesburg, and another daughter, Jade, has recently moved out, but still lives in Cape Town. There is no doubt that this is a very tight-knit family, and a very creative and talented family too.

It's a beautiful, large house standing in a lush garden, with the majestic Table Mountain as a stunning backdrop. From the front door, a long, narrow corridor runs down the middle, with many rooms leading off it. A vast kitchen, a dining room, a couple of living rooms, an office space, and a master bedroom that has a grand en suite bathroom, with glass doors opening out onto a private courtyard. Add to this a second floor with several bedrooms. A porch, a terrace with a pergola, a basement and a number of outbuildings that have been remodelled as cottages complete the property. There is a vegetable garden in the yard outside the kitchen and at the back of the house there is a garden with a swimming pool.

This has been their home for 20 years. When they first saw the house it was the possibilities and the opportunities that it offered that made them fall for it. One thing that strikes me is that this is the first house I have visited here that doesn't have bars in front of the windows. Instead, it has wooden shutters that are closed at night. Security is important in Cape Town, but Doreen doesn't want to live behind bars.

"What is the most important feature in your home?" I ask her.
"The fact that it's wonderful when I'm alone, wonderful when just the family is here and wonderful when there are a hundred guests milling around. The fact that it opens and closes. I never feel lonely here. And I never feel crowded either. It really is a most accommodating house. I wonder if that's the mark of a really good design? Yes, I think that this house is very well

A home is where I feel
me the most.

designed. There are no tricks about it. There isn't anything extraordinary or wow about it. It's just good."

"The light is another thing that I love about it," Doreen continues. "I absolutely love the light. In the mornings when I wake up and I open the shutters one by one, I see how the light falls into the house. I observe how the light comes in at different times of the day. I have favourite places I like to be in as the day progresses and in different seasons. I love to be on this side of the house in the mornings. And in winter I love to be here on the terrace at lunchtime because it's so sunny and lovely. Other spaces offer cool shade from the sun when I need that."

The kitchen plays a central role in this home where cooking and a love of food is obvious. It's large and has a wonderful, homely ambience. The generous tables both in here and in the adjacent dining room, and the many shelves, laden with plates and cooking utensils, testify to meals cooked and shared with friends in abundance.

"Meyer is passionate about cooking and the kitchen garden is his thing," she tells me. "Both my mother and Meyer's mother were great cooks. And I too love to cook and to improvise in the kitchen. But nowadays there are so many cooks in the house that I'd really rather read a book."

 "Do you have a favourite place you like to spend time in?"
"The bedroom. It's my sacred space," she says. "It's where I dream and where
I can fear, where I'm both comfortable and uncomfortable. Here is where
everything happens. My mother always said, 'do something you enjoy every
day'. This space gives me joy every day."

She tells me that she really isn't all that attached to possessions. She loves
both things that are beautiful and things that have a function. "But," she
says, "If I had to choose a favourite piece of furniture, it's definitely the desk
in the bedroom."

She's referring to a beautiful black steel table, designed and made by *Gregor
Jenkin*. It's facing a window in a corner of the bedroom, with a view of the
private courtyard beyond. The light that streams in through the window re-
veals the exquisite texture of the brushed steel surface, and you instinctively
want to run your fingers over it.

"I love the way it looks," she continues "and I love the feeling I get when I'm
sitting at it, and I love what I do there. I work or I write and I create all my
designs at this table."

"How would you describe your interior design style?"
"In the past when I was doing cottages that were to be sold later, it was quite

different. Because I didn't know who was going to live in them it was more like an academic exercise. It was all about form and design and function. This is what I understand and do well. It was easy for me to do, but I was detached.

"Whereas our cottages were planned. It was different doing them in the sense that in contrast to the cottages I did earlier, these cottages are a part of me. They had to have that special element, that kind of soul. But at the same time, that soul can't be too overbearing. It must be accessible. It was quite complicated to do. But the fact that people seem to enjoy and like them is very fulfilling."

"Then, with this house it was about creating a home for us to be comfortable in. I don't think it's particularly well designed. It's more a mishmash, full of things that I have gathered around me and like. I don't like clutter, but at the same time this is a home. So it needs stuff. The older pieces in the house we inherited from our parents. If I buy anything new it's modern. I would say that my style is very simple. Uncomplicated. Pared down."

"Where do you get your inspiration from when you create your home?" "I'm curious," she says. "I am inspired by people's homes and by public spaces. I can get inspiration from magazines, but these days I spend more time online and use *Pinterest*. It's the small things that catch my eye. All the little things that add up to something bigger that inspires me. But I also have a filing system inside my head that is full of stuff. For example I used a red and grey colour scheme in one of our cottages. Years ago I saw an article that made a lasting impact on me. I couldn't remember all the details but I remembered the two colours and their textures. And how they made me feel. So I used that when I designed that cottage."

I stay for a couple of days in one of the cottages on the premises. It's a stunning studio flat with amazing views of the Table Mountain seen through the huge glass facade that wraps itself around the gable of the house. This loft apartment, and in fact the whole hospitality business that Doreen now runs from here, is the result of a leaking roof above their bathroom. When they climbed up to the attic to investigate, they realised the potential of the space. The vistas that could be seen from there. So instead of just repairing the roof they engaged an architect. Together they designed this modern loft extension, because Doreen explains, she wanted it to have a totally different character from the main building that dates from the late 1800s.

Over a lunch on the terrace Doreen tells me a little more about herself. "I understand design," she says. I don't know where that comes from, but I have an inherent feeling for design. I often know that trends are going to develop before they actually happen. I grew up in a beautiful and creative home. My mother was an artist and was always giving lectures in form, balance, colour and composition. And my father was a photographer; I remember spending a lot of time with him in the darkroom."

"I have a Bachelor of Arts in drama from university, and I worked as a publicist for a theatre for a while. I loved that. Then, for many years I worked as a property developer, refurbishing estates. Then I started doing up cottages and that was fun. I could focus more on the interior design and play with things. Like designing wallpaper or working with young designers with exciting ideas.

Then one day, I was approached by the new editor of *Elle Decoration*, and she asked me if I wanted to do a story about a revamp. Because she knew that was what I did. I told her that I would love to do that but I found the prospect nerve-racking because I didn't know anything about the publishing world. And she said 'No, you'll be fine. It might look like a big elephant, but just break the elephant down into small pieces before putting it back together again.' And that was the best advice she could have given me, because that is exactly what it is. So I did just that and I wrote the story. And I think to this day that that was my best story ever. After that I got a new commission and another one after that, and I ended up working with them for six or seven years. And I loved it!"

"But then the editor left and the dynamics changed and also being a stylist is really hard work. Nowadays they have interns who can help out with all the heavy work, but back then there was only me. And then the leaking roof happened. And we knew that the children would leave home in a couple of years and we needed to do something with the house. It's really an incredible house but it doesn't make sense for just Meyer and me to live here by ourselves. We both really like having life and a buzz around us and the house is so fantastic, it gives us enough privacy."

"So, then the cottages just kind of happened. We built them for short-term rentals. I like when people come and go. I like the transience of it. I think that doing the cottages after working with Elle Decoration was a good thing. I had amassed a lot of knowledge by that time. Being there you got exposed to a lot of designers and a lot of products. It was really nice for me to have somewhere to put all of that. So I have used a lot of South African designers in the cottages because I respect what they do, their products are really good and I want to support them as well. Young artists here don't always have the breaks I think they have in Europe. Some of them still live with their parents, because they can't afford to live on their own. And now I'm really keen to have even more cottages because now there are so many new absolutely amazing designers", she says with a twinkle in her eyes.

"There is a large painting hanging on the wall in the cottage I'm staying in. You told me earlier that this came from an artist residency project that you held here. Can you tell me more about that?" I ask Doreen.

"Well, in the winter months it's quieter here," she says. "I wanted to do something that interests me, and that would be of benefit in some way. Last year Cape Town was the World Design Capital. So I did a project with my son, who has an online platform for creatives, and we invited seven artists and designers to come and stay, each for a week. Their brief was to create a unique piece inspired by their surroundings and by the Mother City. I didn't expect anything from them. It was more to give them the space to do something, than it was to get something out of it. Two of the works were later exhibited at *Iziko,* which is our national museum. One of the artists was *Michael Chandler.* He was inspired by the Cape heritage, and his contribution was this impressive replica of a traditional *V.O.C.* dish, *Verenigde Oostindische Compagnie* or *Dutch East India Company,* using chalk on paper."

And Doreen has since then cleverly changed the interior design of the cottage to match this piece of art. Picking up the blue colour on some of the walls, and having similar blue patterned plates and other details that match, all with her skilful eye for design.

"We were so inspired," she continues, "so next year we want to do this again." Another event that creates a buzz in the house is the *Food Jams* that their daughter Jade regularly hosts from the family kitchen. It all started when she attended university. She is a talented jazz musician, a saxophonist, but inspired by her family's love of food and cooking, she entered the first Masterchef South Africa and made it all the way to the finals. Back at university, her fellow students and new friends wanted her to cook for them because she was so good at it. But she had grown to understand the role that food plays in bringing people together. And how cooking with other people is half the fun of sharing a meal. So she said 'No, let's do it together.' And so the Food Jams were born.

On my first day here in their home, she is preparing for a Food Jam. She organizes different stations in the big kitchen. While I'm taking photographs in the house, people arrive. Soon there are sounds of music playing and laughter, and before long they are cooking up a storm in the kitchen. Watching it all come together is such a kick, that I'm eager to take part in one myself before I leave Cape Town. And I get to do so with some new friends I made here and a few people that I never met before. Before the evening was over I felt we were friends for life. This is the beauty of cooking together. Jade's idea with the Food Jams unites people regardless of background, circumstances or walks of life.

This pretty much sums up what this place is all about. Not just a warm and inviting home. But also a home where interesting people meet, and where wondrous things are created.

"Do you have a motto in life?"
'Don't sweat the small stuff.' "That means don't be bothered about things that are inconsequential. I think it's important to realize what's important. If something is important for you then by all means do it, but if it isn't, then

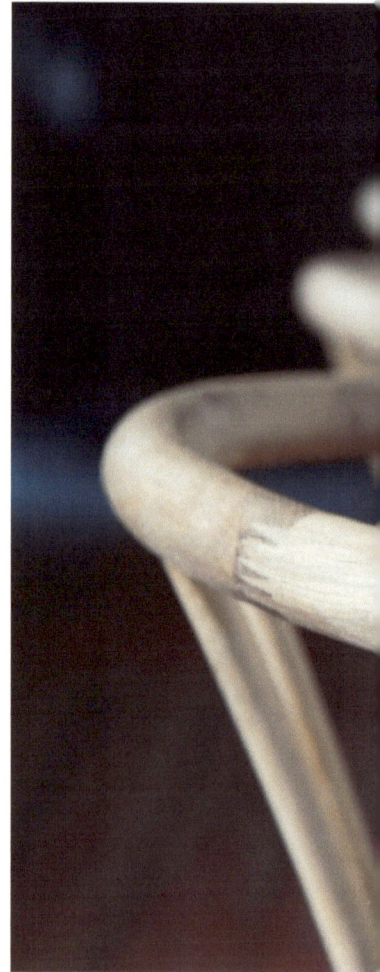

don't worry about it, just let it go. This is an insight that comes with age I think."

"What is the best advice you would give to people when it comes to creating a home for themselves?"
"Trust yourself and be yourself," she says. "Do what you like and not just what you think other people will like. If you do that with integrity, even if it's whacky and weird, if it's you, it will be wonderful. Don't be scared to trust yourself."

"What would your dream home be if you didn't live here?"
"It would be very basic and simple, nearly monastic, with lots of light. I would love that. Not have too much stuff. It would only have one room, a living space with a kitchen and one bedroom. And that would be it. There would be eight plates, and eight knives and forks. Very pared down and very simple. What I would do there? Meditate. Do yoga more. Have time to sit in the sun. Chat. Be with friends. Spend time with Meyer which I love doing. Spend time with me that I love doing. This is my vision and dream."

"What does a home mean to you?"
"A home is where I feel me the most. It's where I feel the most comfortable. Where I can dream. And be with people that I care for. I can also feel me, when I'm on a beach by myself, or if I'm walking in the mountains. But I think that home is the safest place where I feel me the most."

ERIKA

LA CONDESA, MEXICO CITY

Erika Krutzfeldt
Graphic Designer
Interior Designer

HEALING SPACES

LA CONDESA, MEXICO CITY

Erika Krutzfeldt is a graphic designer and interior designer, and she lives in La Condesa, Mexico City. She shares her home with her cat Keiju, a Finnish name that means fairy. *'Feel free to do whatever you want, but with moderation'* is advice that was passed on to her by her father and has now become a motto she tries to live by.

Born in Mexico, Erika spent ten years living in La Paz, Bolivia with her family before returning to Mexico. She studied graphic design at the University of Guadalajara for five years and started working as one after that. Two years ago she went to Barcelona and studied interior design at a design school for one year.

"When I came back I went to an astrologer," she tells me. "The astrologer was a very old woman who lives here in Mexico City. She told me that I had a gift for healing spaces. That inspired me so much that my next project is going to be using this concept. Healing spaces to me means to create well-being. By freeing up spaces, rearranging objects, regrouping, adding or removing pieces, you can create a whole new way of perceiving a space. A home is a state of the soul."

Her way of arranging her own furniture and decorating her apartment sets a good example. The furniture is not routinely aligned with the walls. Instead the living room furniture is angled, making the room look both interesting and inviting. A distinct feature is the warm yellow colour on the rear wall that stops abruptly a bit into the adjacent wall. This colour is actually just a continuation of the patio wall on the other side of the large floor-to-ceiling window, and painting the living room wall in the same shade makes these two spaces interconnect.

The yellow colour continues in the small dining room next to the kitchen. But here only in the ceiling making it feel like the sun is shining from above, which is beneficial in this slightly darker, south facing area. To enhance the impression of sunshine, the ceiling lamp above the dining table is an Asian parasol, traditionally used to give shade from the sun. Ornaments and objects are grouped aesthetically around the apartment.

equivalent to 1076 square feet

A mirror on the wall reflects the light. Hard surfaces balance against soft. Bare spaces against more cluttered.

As Erika works from home and has her office at one end of the large living room, she has divided the space with floor-to-ceiling drapes. When work ends on Fridays, she pulls the drapes to conceal the work area. By shutting it off visually, she mentally closes her mind from work.

It was the neighborhood that first drew her here. Everything important was happening around La Condesa, and when her best friend who was living here moved out of her apartment, Erika moved in.

"I really like the layout of it," she says. "It feels even more spacious than the 100 square meters* it is. And I also like the old wooden floors that give it such a warm feeling. The patios are also wonderful to have when the weather's warm. Then I have barbecues out there with my friends. When I'm alone I like to be in my bedroom because it's so cosy. And when I have friends over, we mostly sit on the large cushions on the floor in the living room."

"I love travelling," she says. "It's a great inspiration and an interest that I have. I also love second-hand things so flea markets are a must."

Erika's belongings testify to her love of other cultures. She has objects from the Middle East, Asia and from other parts of Latin America. The floor cushions are from Peru, Morocco and Uzbekistan. A large table lamp, which is a favourite of hers, comes from Asia. Several old artefacts are Mexican.

"My style could best be described as colourful and folkloristic, in the sense of crafted things of mixed of origins," she says. "And I like furniture from the 50s and have quite a few pieces from that era. I like crafts and old things that have a soul. What I don't like is mass-produced things that have come directly from a factory, but things that have had a previous life and have a story to tell."

"Where do you get your inspiration from?"
"From travelling definitely. I visit a lot of hotels. Earlier I used to find inspiration in magazines. But at school they drummed into us: 'No more *Architectural Digest*!' They wanted us to see beyond trends and were great believers in classical and timeless design. But I'm decorative by nature. I want to have all these things around me to give me inspiration. I think my apartment really reflects who I am."

"What would your dream home be if you didn't live here?"
"It would be a beach house in Tulum in the Caribbean part of Mexico. That particular area is known for its cenotes. They are great sinkholes in the ground filled with water, like amazing underground swimming pools. The house would be of stone and have different levels. It doesn't have to have

equivalent to 1076 square feet

—*A home is a place where I feel safe. Where I have confidence.*

views of the sea because I love the jungle and would prefer to have a jungle view."

"What does a home mean to you?"
"Home is the most important place. I love to travel but I love even more to come home. It's a place where I feel safe. Where I have confidence. It's comfortable and harmonious. It's simply perfect and nothing is missing."

EYAL

SHEUNG WAN, HONG KONG

Eyal Cohen
COO in a financial Asset Management

THE COSY HOME IN NO 4

SHEUNG WAN, HONG KONG

A couple of floors up a steep and narrow staircase in an apartment building in Sheung Wan, Hong Kong, I find the home of Eyal Cohen. The house is what the Chinese call a 'walk-up', a building from the 50-60s with no elevator. The first thing I see as I step inside is a bright and colourful wall made of – egg cartons. It's a cheering and welcoming sight and a real work of art.

Eyal, originally from Israel, works as a COO in a financial asset management and his work and personal life have taken him around the world, to places like London, Cyprus, Tokyo, and Sydney. Since he has always lived in a constant transition between countries, cities and rented and furnished apartments, this is actually the first time he has made a home for himself.

His apartment is fairly spacious for Hong Kong, 575 square feet* and consists of one large room, a kitchen and a bathroom. It's furnished and decorated by himself and filled with fun and eye-catching things. One wall has an image of a large ostrich with a hat. A full-scale sheep with blue wool is standing on top of a bookshelf. Origami squirrels are playing on a tree trunk on the floor. This is a home whose owner clearly has had a lot of fun whilst decorating it and I'm eager to hear the story behind it.

"Rental apartments here in Hong Kong are usually small and furnished," he tells me. "Since I always have lived in furnished apartments that are purely functional, I was happy to find that this one was empty. Because this meant that I could create a place that resonates more with myself. A place I could put my heart into. I loved the tiled floors with the industrial imperfect feeling. They manufactured shoes here at one time."

"Was the fact that it was unfurnished the main reason you chose it?"
"Yes and also the space versus the cost. I managed to get it for a very reasonable price. The light was also a factor. The living room windows are large and the sunlight comes in indirectly from the building across the street. And the location of course was important. I wanted to live in this area as my friends all live within one kilometre radius. We eat out as default, so cooking and having people over is a novelty in central Hong Kong. I'm pleased to have the space now so that friends can come over."

*equivalent to 53,5 square metres

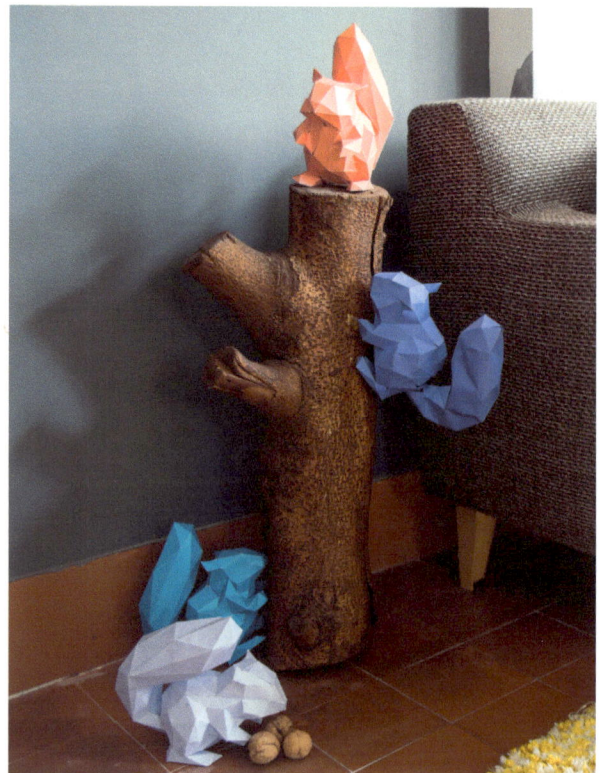

I want to know if the moderate price had anything to do with the number four that is part of the address? I had heard about this number being un-favourable in this part of the world. Eyal confirms this. The number four is considered very unlucky as it has the same sound as the word for death. As Chinese people are very superstitious, this number doesn't exist in places like elevators. And if this wasn't enough, there is a coffin shop on the ground floor and this apparently is bad Feng Shui. Adding to this is the fact that it was here in Sheung Wan that the bubonic plague started around 1890. All this together will do nothing to increase property value for the locals. But all in all it turned out to be very fortunate for Eyal.

"Tell me about your ideas about furnishing and decorating your home?" "This is a large room and I wanted to have a secluded space as a bedroom and I needed storage for my clothes. I came up with the solution to create a wall with cupboards to make a bedroom on one side and have a hallway on the other side. Then I went to the market and picked up egg cartons and covered the entire back of the cupboards with them. As I love colour I paint-ed them with acrylic paint in different hues and added lighting on the top to enhance the effect. As I wanted to somewhat obscure the bed, I positioned a bookshelf as a fourth wall and this made the bedroom semi secluded."

Living here means that you are able to inherit furniture when people move away. The table, dining chairs and a bookcase are such inherited items from people leaving Hong Kong. But the sofa is brand new, and the rug too, cho-sen for its colours that match the floor tiles. The rest he has created himself. He built the coffee table out of picture frames and the egg carton theme continues here too.

"I make it up as I go along," he says. "Take the boxes on the wall. Since I like wine, I had these empty wine boxes and I started to think what I could do with them. I like to collect small things that I call *cutesy-stuff*. Some of them go back to my childhood. And especially since going to Japan for many years, with all their cute and cool small things they have there, I have a collection of cutesy-stuff. So I decorated the wine boxes with these, each with it's own story. One is about my grandparents. My granddad was ob-sessed with cars. Another one has my parents in it. It's just for fun, recreating a memory of happy times."

One can be led to believe that it's all about fun and upbeat feelings in the décor, but Eyal also talks about the importance of creating a balance be-tween fun and sombre. In amongst the cute things is for example a painting poster featuring a Swedish artist, *Peter Tillberg*. The photorealistic painting it features is called 'Are you profitable little friend?' implying for who are you profitable? It shows young pupils with grey faces sitting at their desks in straight rows, seen from a slightly elevated position, as previously used when taking class photos.

—A home is a place that is cosy for myself. A place where I put my heart.

"The blue sheep I got from an exhibition. It was just after the Chinese calendar's *'Year of the Sheep'* new years celebrations ended. The small installation with the squirrels began when I found a piece of wood in the street. I then purchased the origami squirrels design and thought they would go well together. I had to assemble them myself, and it seemed to take forever. But I find that I like the craft side of decorating. It's quite the opposite of what I do at work, that requires a more technical skill", he continues.

"How would you describe your interior design style?"
"Eclectic cosy? I like to have a balance between cute and sombre, but at the end of the day it has to a place that is comfortable for me."

"Where do you get your inspiration from?"
"I have a daughter with two women who are very close friends from Tel Aviv and they inspire me. They are both designers and live in Sydney, and have made themselves a great home from what once was a garage. I go there once a month to be with my daughter. I also appreciate the boldness of colour. When I get an idea, it's all about trying and testing, working out how to make things colourful in a nice way, not flamboyant for it's own sake."

"What is your favourite colour if you had to choose one?"
"I would say green," he says. "Maybe it has got something to do with coming from an arid country, with more desert than greenery. The Cacti I have here remind me of home."

"What is the best advice you can give people in terms of making a home for themselves?"
"Have fun! Synthesize what you like and what appeals to you and create your own mix to make your home resonate with you."

"What would your dream home be if you didn't live here?"
"I don't have a dream home as such. Perhaps it would be to have a few homes in different places. Places that meant a lot to me. Like Sydney where my daughter lives, and Tel Aviv where I grew up and London where I lived for eleven years and where I have still have many friends. Different places give you different things. Maybe having a home in each of these places would be a way of bringing together all the facets of my life?"

"What does a home mean to you?"
"A home is very special to me. It's more than only a place where all my things are. When I walk through my door, I feel very comfortable. Surrounded by my things, arranged in a way that arouses different feelings in me, it's a place that is cosy for myself. A place where I put my heart."

EMILY

MANHATTAN, NEW YORK

Emily Johnston
Artist
Photographer

CONSCIOUSLY MINIMAL

MANHATTAN, NEW YORK

Emily Johnston, an artist and photographer has her home in East Village, Manhattan.

"I feel very fortunate that what I'm passionate about is what I get to do at work," she tells me. "Which is about understanding the world and my place in the world by making images."

"I'm often struck by different passages and quotations," she answers me when I ask her if she has any motto she lives by. She takes out a small card where she has written down an excerpt from the American poet John Ashbery: *'I thought that if I could put it all down, that would be one way, and then the thought came to me, that to leave it all out, would be another and truer way'.* "This is only one of many quotations like this one that I usually keep around my studio when I work. They tend to draw out different things in me and bring another context to what I'm doing."

Her apartment is stylishly furnished throughout in muted shades and has a calm and harmonious ambience.

"What I really liked about this apartment when I saw it for the first time, was that it had a space I could use as an office, and that the living room had doors and is separate. As I work from home it's really important to find ways to make a separation between work and relaxation. I determined that the living room was a place I wouldn't work in, but would be where I could relax, read and think. I like the layout of this place too. You can be in the kitchen and another person can be in the living room and you feel like you are in a completely different space, which is a nice feature for such a small apartment."

She has been living in her 450 square feet* apartment for about four years. Before discovering this apartment she visited nearly a hundred other ones, finding most of them dark and depressing. This one was light and airy with windows in every room. "With daylight in all the rooms I feel the passing of time and the qualities that brings," she clarifies.

The bedroom is in a tiny alcove tucked away in the passage between the

*equivalent to 42 square metres

kitchen and office space. There is a large window here too but the ceiling-to-floor drapes in front of the bed makes this space very private. The dark grey walls enhance the cosy feeling. "There isn't a wasted space of a separate bedroom which is another thing I really like here," she says.

"The building is from the late 1800s but the spaces have been defined and re-defined many times over the years, and I appreciate the character it has. When I moved in I decided to go with all different shades of grey and applied this throughout the apartment. The kitchen is in a very pale grey, except one wall that is dark grey. This was actually an accident, due to a mis-communication with my painter, but it turned out to be a happy accident, because I like it. Initially I wanted to paint the apartment in progressively darker shades. The office has a dark shade, but I decided to make the living room lighter, because I wanted to be drawn towards the brighter spaces."

"Where is your favourite area, where you spend most of your time?"
"The most peaceful space is in the living room. The light in here is so beautiful," she says. "This is where I have my books and I like to sit here and think. And then I can notice a book and pull it out and rediscover it. I like to almost pretend that I'm a guest in my own home when I'm in my living room and explore a little bit."

"Do you have a favourite piece of furniture?"
"I really like the Tom Dixon table in the kitchen. It was probably the first design purchase I made. I had loved this table for a long time and when I moved from Chicago to New York I bought this table. It's such a great piece and I love how flexible it is. In a future home, if it's larger, it could be lowered and become a coffee table. I like the surface of it, how marble ages and gets worn."

"How would you describe your interior design style?"
I feel that I'm at a stage in my life when my home doesn't match my style. Though it's not so much a question of style. It's not that I prefer one aesthetic over another aesthetic. It's got more to do with myself and that I'm changing. If I had to redo my home again, it would be much simpler. I'm much more inclined now to minimize any visual distraction. Because I find that my most creative and productive times are when there is nothing on the walls. When light is allowed to move through rooms because there aren't a lot of objects to catch the eye. What I think I need now is a more meditative visual experience, uncluttered by specific items.

When I was working as a commercial photographer and doing editorial work, I was working on my own projects too, though not in a very focused way. At that time my home was a very important form of personal expression. But I realise now that the crafting and composing of my home, was a bit of a replacement for the crafting and composing of my own projects.

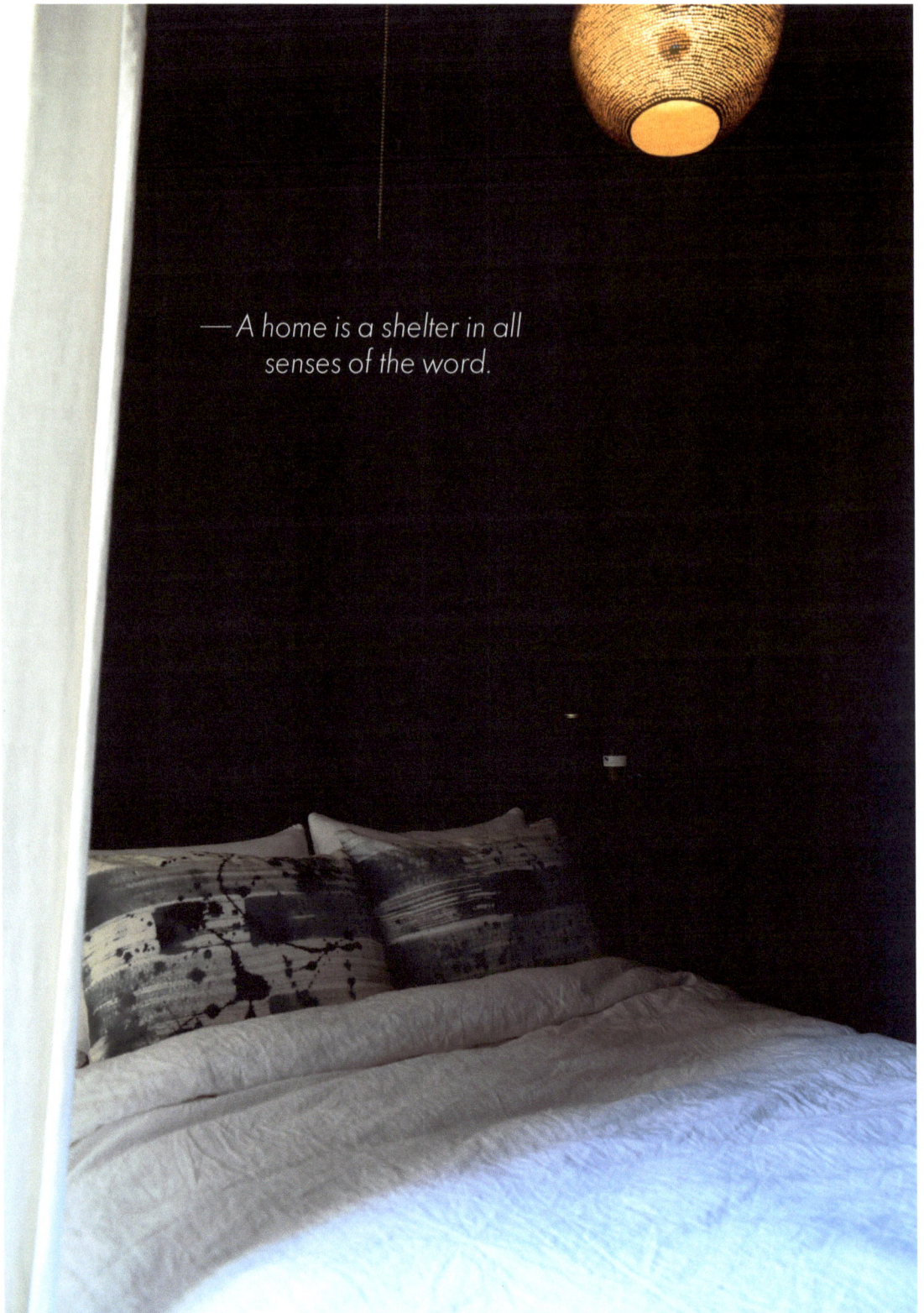

*—A home is a shelter in all
senses of the word.*

As my own work started to develop, I found that I wanted my home to be less expressive and more neutral. Today I think a lot about what I want my next space to be like, or how I can redo this place if I stay here. I think about space now in more sculptural terms; I think architectural is technically the term to use. About the structure more than what I'm going to put in it. Of creating a box to hold my different processes rather than a box containing my things. So my style would be best described as consciously minimal, in order to focus and to expand myself in a creative way."

"Where did you get your inspiration from when you created this home?"
"From things I see everywhere. In looking at lots of different homes, artist studios, and magazines. Generally looking at the way people conceive their spaces. And then mix different impressions and not apply one specific style. Asking myself, what makes sense for me? I like cooking, so I like the open shelving in the kitchen because the way I like to cook is like having a palette. I see what I have and can compose my meals with what I see on the shelves."

"Do you think that your home reflects who you are?"
"My work is shifting and I'm eager to rearrange my home too, but I'm not ready to do that yet. So yes, I think my home reflects tremendously who I am. So much so that the fact that I'm changing makes me want to change it. It's obviously a very strong reflection of who I am and who I have been."

"What is the best advice you can give people in terms of making a home for themselves?"
"To think first about what you want your home to be for you. I believe most people approach decorating or arranging their home by trying to make it aesthetically perfect, following a code or a style.

It's always been very important for me to think more in terms of: Where am I going to want to sit in the morning? Where is the nicest light going to be? Where am I going to enjoy what this space offers the most? And after that, thinking about placing things there. Really try to make a home for yourself. A home that puts you in the mindset that you want to live your life in. That adds to your life. And not look upon it solely as a functional space, like a place to sit and a place to eat. Try to think more in terms of how you can arrange things to bring joy to your life."

"What would your dream home be if you didn't live here?"
"Right now, although I have never been there myself, it is the home of *Georgia O'Keeffe* in the desert of New Mexico that would be my dream home. I like the simplicity of it. The materials it's made of – wood and adobe, and the feeling as if it's made of only one piece. It's very pared down, rustic and simple and has a sculptural feeling. And living close to nature is also very appealing to me. To be able to move inside and outside in a seamless way."

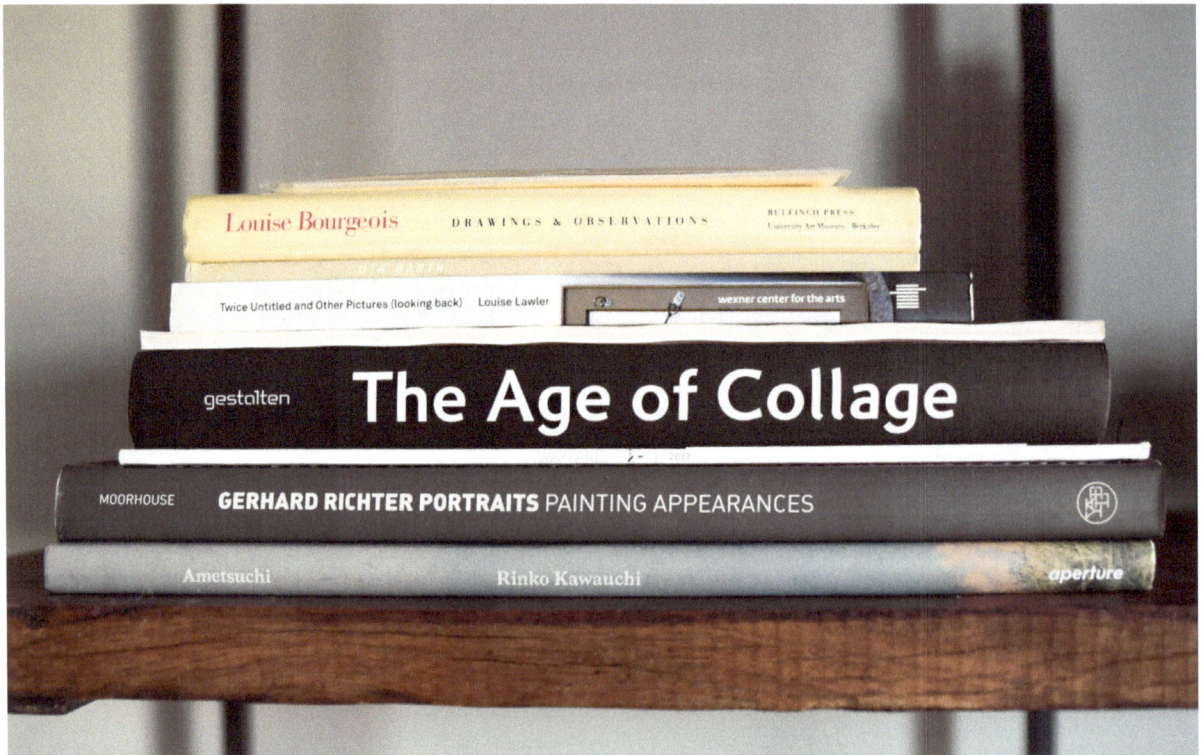

"What does a home mean to you?"
"It's a shelter in all senses of the word. A shelter primarily from the environ-ment, but also from the human environment, especially if you live like I do in a big city. As a creative person I feel it's important to create a safe haven in the midst of it. It's protection, security but also emotional protection. We all create a world that makes us feel safe."

CARIN

GREEN POINT, CAPE TOWN

Carin Lilienfeld
Consultant in publishing

LOVE OF COLOURS

GREEN POINT, CAPE TOWN

I arrive at Carin's home straight from Asia. Stepping through the front door into a room full of vivid colours, bold patterns, face masks and artefacts, I immediately feel that I'm in Africa. Her home is a small Victorian town-house in Green Point. The house has a discreet grey façade, but is vibrant with colours inside. A living room on the ground floor opens up all the way to the rafters, with a kitchen to one side. Two bedrooms, a bathroom and an enclosed courtyard swathed in greenery are also on this floor. Tucked away under the eaves is her bedroom that also has a small workspace and a second bathroom.

At first she shared the house with her youngest daughter but now both of her daughters have their own homes. There is also a granddaughter now and her family visits her regularly. The bedrooms are used these days for visiting friends and she rents them out occasionally as well. Having house guests is something she thoroughly enjoys.

Carin is a freelancer, often working from home with photo and copyright research for publishers. Her background as a textile designer shows up in the strong colours and prominent patterns found in her home. She is also educated in art and painting and plans to return to it one day. The paints and brushes are ready and waiting. But it's in interior decoration where she mostly finds an outlet for her creativity today. It may be by painting a piece of furniture or a staircase, sewing cushion covers or by upcycling things. She is true to her motto, which is: *'It's the doing and the loving of the doing that brings happiness'.*

When she bought the house five years ago, it was the openness and airiness of it that attracted her. The interior, which was painted white and had a clean appearance, was another essential factor. The size was also right, about 90 square meters*, as she was keen to downsize. Her daughters suggested at first that she move to an apartment, but she felt she needed an outside space too.

"The house felt secure," she says. "Because this area was new to me and I felt that I was out of my comfort zone, this was an important aspect."

She moved in and the decorating could begin. What wasn't already white

*equivalent to 969 square feet

she painted white, before she began to pour in colour. When she describes the house, as it was when she bought it, it comes across as a blank canvas just waiting for her to put her stamp on it.

"Show me anything that can't be painted," she says. I love playing with paint and I had a lot of fun when I painted the furniture, the doors and the staircase. My favourite colours are red, yellow and turquoise, especially when they are combined with white."

"How would you describe your interior design style?"
"My style is very simple, almost naïve, and colourful. I have no rules whatsoever. If I like something I will buy it, but it would always have to be cheap. My biggest thrill is to do something cheaply and to upcycle things. It gives me more pleasure than buying something new and expensive."

"Take the bannister for example. There wasn't anything on the wall for support, when going up and down the stairs, so I needed to do something. I always have an eye open when I'm out on walks and I was searching for a branch that had the right dimensions that could work as a handrail. It took some time to find, but one day on a walk in the forest I found it. And with a lick of paint I had my bannister. Wherever I am, I always tend to collect things. Not fancy or expensive things but everyday objects, many found on the beach or in the forest, from junk shops and markets. I suppose I suffer from the *'irrepressible urge to decorate my surroundings'*.

—A home is a place where I can be alone. Free to be just me.

"Kaffe Fassett said something that I think very fittingly describes me," she says. *'The irrepressible urge in some people to decorate their surroundings is a never-ending fascination to me. Like them I am incapable of living in a plain unadorned space for more than a day or two. A postcard, a leaf, a bit of fabric, feathers, soon arrange themselves on my walls.'*

"Where do you get your inspiration from?"
"I get my inspiration from everywhere really, from magazines, books, or from other people's homes. I love eclectic things, African beadwork, strong designs and primary colours. To help me organise ideas I keep scrapbooks. I'll tear out anything from magazines that I like and put them in flip files. But I only keep things that are really meaningful to me. Then maybe years later I find ideas that I can use. I have several books. One for plants and gardens, one for furniture and so on."

"What is the best advice you can give people in terms of making a home for themselves?"
"Be true to what you really like, and not what you think will impress others," she answers. "I can walk into houses that are really nice, decorated in greens and browns. But I just can't make my own home like that. Try to make your home in your own style and in a way that really appeals to you. Perhaps

making scrapbooks as I do could be good advice. In making them, take anything that inspires you; it can be a colour, a shape, or a pattern. Collect inspiration even though it doesn't feel relevant to you at the time. As long as it resonates with you, it's good."

We are seated in the courtyard having this chat. It's a tranquil space with walls on three sides covered in greenery, with vibrant red doors, leading to storage spaces, in stark contrast to the foliage. The roof is made up of evenly spaced branches painted white, creating an airy trellis. There is a soothing sound from a small fountain nestled in the ivy on the back wall. When Carin moved in, the yard was totally bare, but she could see that she could transform it into a beautiful space. The glass wall with the sliding door that covers the entire opening into the living room, allows the light to flow in and makes the interior and exterior areas merge into one.

"In the winter I cut everything back to get as much light as possible. And in the summer I let it grow as much as possible to create shade from the sun," she tells me. "Then the ivy and the star jasmine cover the branches above and form a roof."

"Where is your favourite area, where you spend most time?"
"I spend a lot of time working upstairs in my office, but I like to sit out here too. Especially in summertime when I entertain friends, we usually tend to sit here. In wintertime I enjoy being on the sofa on the front porch catching the sun. Here I have a small garden of cacti and stonecrop, which is what gives that side of the house a totally different character than the courtyard. Overall it's a very comfortable house to live in."

"What do you love most about your home?"
"I love the sense of privacy I have here. I'm in the middle of the city, but when I close the front door, I'm in my own little space."

"What would your dream home be if you didn't live here?"
"It would be a little cottage in the countryside with a big garden, with chickens, vegetables and fruit trees. I envision it as similar to this house but more rustic and simple. It would have a big fireplace, which is the only thing I miss having here. In wintertime it would be wonderful to have a fire burning in a hearth. It would be useful too as this house doesn't have central heating."

"What does a home mean to you?"
"It's a place where I can be alone, free to be just me. Surrounded by the things that matter to me. I could be happy in a smaller place too, and I can easily get rid of more things as well, as long as I have a door that I can close."

ELISSA

EAST WILLIAMSBURG, NEW YORK

Elissa Ehlin
Enamelist

WABI SABI IN BROOKLYN

EAST WILLIAMSBURG, NEW YORK

East Williamsburg in Brooklyn is an area that's becoming more residential as factories and warehouses move out. This is where Elissa Ehlin lives, and she shares her home with her husband Jay Leritz, Cougar their son, and their cat Pretty Perfect.

The low-rise buildings around their home are covered in imaginative graffiti by internationally renowned street artists, and theirs is no different. They have lived here for eight years and have transformed what previously was an auto repair workshop in an industrial building into a very personal home. The extensive construction work that this has required, they did themselves with the help of friends.

Elissa is an enamelist by profession like her husband, and they have one of their two studios in the same building. This atmospheric home has exposed wood beams, brick walls and metal beams, wooden floors, rustic plank stairs and a serene colour scheme. It's set up on two levels with an open plan living room and kitchen on one floor. A mid-century conical fireplace is in one corner of the room. Lying on the floor next to it is a large dove-grey floor cushion that acts as a sofa and a Pioneer chair. Handmade objects adorn shelves, walls and table surfaces. There is a large roof deck upstairs and on the ground floor are the bedrooms.

Nothing in this home is mass-produced. On the contrary, everything here is made either by themselves or by people they know. Every single object has been carefully chosen and is a cherished and loved possession.

"I'm passionately interested in American craft and handicraft. Everything we have is handmade down to the bedding that's hand woven and of a high quality. And I myself only wear the clothes of two designers. I'd rather live with nothing till I get what I want," Elissa says.

Their home is very consciously thought out and there are very good reasons why it needs to be as subdued as it is, she tells me. One of them is the city of New York itself. The pressure of living in such a fast-paced and stressful environment, where nobody walks fast enough and where even the simplest of tasks can be overwhelming, takes its toll.

"My home needs to feel restorative," she says. "When I come home I feel like I can breathe."

Another reason is that Elissa sits on the board of *The color Association of the United States*. The board members bring different areas of experience within the industry and they forecast colour trends three years in advance.

"My expertise is in the handcrafted and handmade. We make colour presentations all year round. This means that I'm thinking about colours constantly. When I'm surrounded by a calm and neutral palette, it allows me to focus on what I'm working out in my head for our next big presentation."

Her motto is *'Love and aesthetics.'* She loves loving her family and her friends she tells me. And she loves aesthetics because every time she looks at something she wants it to be beautiful. But it doesn't have to be perfect by any means, emphasizes Elissa.

"I'm not looking for perfect standards. I live with so many imperfections. But I can relate to the Japanese philosophy *wabi sabi**, an aesthetic described as a beauty that is imperfect, impermanent, and incomplete. In my experience we love or value things up until a certain point. After it has peaked, our interest usually starts to wane. I'm interested in the perceived values of that specific phase when things start to fade or die. This is when we usually throw away or discard them."

"This applies to people as well. In our culture people become invisible after a certain age. Age is simply not appreciated here. Jay and I don't value trends. We totally lack that need to upgrade. There is a sustainable element in this from Jay's perspective, as he approaches his work with a sustainable mindset. But I love crafts and handicraft for their own sake."

Everything she has, she has bought out of love for its design, shape and aesthetic: objects that are handmade and that can withstand age and trends and still remain beautiful. But she also has a very personal relationship with her belongings. When she looks at her teapot, she sees not only the teapot but *Alex Marshall*, the ceramist. And when she looks at her black handmade bowls she actually sees *Yumiko Kuga* who made them, in her mind's eye. Because they are so obviously present to her, one can, in a sense say that she's surrounded not only by things but by friends in her home.

"When we had our financial collapse in 2008, it was the best thing that could have happened to me from a philosophical standpoint, even though we were completely affected by it. We had to shut down our business and let all our employees go, because orders stopped coming in. Our bank went down and it was a large national bank. As horrible as it was while it was going on, I came out of it as a changed person. The crises forced me to have an honest conversation with myself about what was really going on in my

— Home is my family.
They are my passion.
My everything.

life. I gained a deeper understanding of my values and beliefs. It changed my approach to money. I realized just how valuable family is. It also made home very important. I value it more. It changed my lifestyle and I'm grateful for everything I have now."

They had just moved in here at that time, from another house across the street. They had the same landlord then as they have now, and he thought that this house would be a better place for the family. We developed the building for him and filled it up with other tenants like the restaurant and bar around the corner, she tells me.

"What feature do you like most in your home? Where do you spend most of your time?"
"The wooden beams in the ceiling and the fireplace for sure. And as I love Chinese food and cooking I spend a lot of my time in the kitchen. We have travelled extensively to China over the years, when Jay worked as a consultant, designing products."

"Do you have a favourite piece of furniture and, if so, why?"
"I absolutely love our bed. And I love the weekend that we found the tree that we used for the bed. Jay milled that tree into planks and planed it into a beautiful headboard. I love the whole lifecycle of that. I'm thrilled every time I look at it."

"How would you describe your interior design style?"
"Handcrafted modern. Handcraft has deep roots, but has always been frowned upon. Art and design have always been well regarded, while handcraft has been in a grey zone. But now handcraft in America is very modern. Not modern as in contemporary design but modern as in fresh."

"Where do you get your inspiration from?"
"I love the Japanese wabi sabi aesthetic. I also like the clean wood element of Scandinavian design. We enjoy spending our leisure time camping, fishing and canoeing. Nature is essential to us, and I like to bring in elements of nature into our home. I'm also inspired by our friends, all of whom are extremely talented. I know everybody who has made everything in my house. Jay and my friends inspire me the most, I would say."

"What advice would you give others in making a home for themselves?"
"Don't settle too quickly. A home is not necessarily made instantly. I think of it more as crafting a home. Personal style isn't just limited to your external appearance. It's about your home too. Your personal style should translate into your home. For me a home represents a beautiful life. I'm very particular of what I bring into it. I not only love for example this piece of glass that holds my water. I care for the person who made it and I like knowing where it came from. I prefer to buy things from my friends and directly impact on

their life positively, than to benefit an unknown manufacturer. You have to have a relationship with everything in your home. So let it take time and choose things that you really love. And don't be hard on yourself, because nothing can be perfect."

"What would your dream home be if you didn't live here?"
"We would love to live close to nature and to be able to live near a river. Jay and I will eventually buy a piece of property in the woods and build our own cabin. It would be a wood cabin but with natural stone work too. It would definitely have a fireplace as I love heating with wood. We are looking for this in areas like upstate New York, western Massachusetts or in Pennsylvania. But it would be a second home to use on weekends and in the summertime because I love living here in New York."

"What does a home mean to you?"
"Home is my family. It's Cougar and Jay. And the cat. They are my passion. My everything."

Wabi Sabi is a Japanese philosophy that embraces the transience of life, whether nature's seasonal changes, the different phases of human existence: childhood, youth, middle age and old age or the imperfections found in objects. Wabi sabi expresses simplicity, humility, unpretentiousness and an understanding that everything is constantly changing and nothing is permanent. The concept of wabi sabi subtly conveys a sense of peaceful melancholy and spiritual longing. Wabi sabi invites us to appreciate the beauty of the imperfect, impermanent, and incomplete in our physical world.

PAULINA

SAN ÁNGEL, MEXICO CITY

Paulina Parlange Pizarro
Business owner
Biologist

THE MURALIST'S HOME

SAN ÁNGEL, MEXICO CITY

Paulina Parlange Pizarro is French/Mexican, a biologist by profession and a business owner in textiles. Her company works with indigenous women in Mexico and supports them in designing, marketing and exporting their creations, according to fair trade rules. She has lived in Mexico City all her life, but has travelled around Mexico since she was very young, and believes that her interest in textiles and in the production of artwork for utilitarian uses started at an early age through these travels.

"My work has always been my passion," she says. "I love every aspect of the production of textiles. But I also take great pleasure in the way it has made it possible for me to travel to the most remote places and to get to know different kinds of people. The historical and cultural background of this country is so interesting and varied. My focus in working with textiles is to understand the context in which they are produced. To be aware of how the communities work. And to appreciate the enormous skill of these artisans, whose knowledge has been passed on from generation to generation. The elderly have a very active part in these communities, something that is disappearing in the modern world. My mission, together with my business partner, is to preserve the old craft techniques of Mexico, so they will not disappear."

Paulina lives in the former home of *Juan O'Gorman*, the Irish/Mexican artist and architect, famous for his murals and mosaics. His most well known work is the *UNAM University Library of Mexico City*, and the *Bank of Mexico*. The façade of the Library is covered in mosaics of natural stones with motifs of the Mexican people's history. Very different are the houses he designed for his friends, Diego Rivera and Frida Kahlo, just two streets away. These buildings, from 1933, are in a functionalist style people called brutalist-functionalism at the time. They were the very first of their kind in the city and were very controversial. He had first designed and built this very house in the same functionalist style, originally for his father but it was later to become his own home.

Paulina has lived in this house for close to 30 years. It was a coincidence that she bought it. Her grandparents lived close by and she happened to stroll by one day after visiting them, at the same time as the gardener was about to leave

and they began to talk. It was through him that she learned that the house was for sale. She fell in love with it as soon as she saw it, and the fact that it was a large enough to accommodate a family with five children made it perfect. Fortunately for them, O'Gorman hadn't reached the height of fame he received later. He was mainly known as a painter at that time. Later, an architect's research revealed that he had had contact with *Le Corbusier* and *Gaudi* through letters where they shared ideas about modernism. This re-established him as an architect and made this house famous in the process.

Today her children are all grown up and have flown the nest and she is divorced from their father. She lives here with her dog Luna and uses parts of the house for her company. The former library with its high ceiling and built-in bookshelves is now a showroom and also where she stores the textiles.

The living room has a ceiling height of nearly six metres. It has a stunning floor-to-ceiling window that takes in the greenery of the garden and the adjoining blocks of blood red and cobalt blue on the different parts of the buildings that make up the house. This large room was built on the existing house and where Juan O'Gorman had his studio. And it's here that Paulina spends the most of her time.

Our conversation takes an unexpected turn when she points out of the window and tells me: "He hanged himself out there in that tree!" It turned out that O'Gorman committed suicide in 1982 at the age of 76, with great drama as he hanged, shot and poisoned himself at the same time.

More amazing still, it turns out that Juan O'Gorman's spirit is still present in this home. The old gardener was the one who told her this and that he still had conversations with him frequently. And it happens from time to time that people who visit her claim to have seen or perceived him. A friend, a female doctor who was visiting, asked her when she was coming back from visiting the bathroom: "Is that your grandfather?" "Who?" Paulina wondered. "The old man that's in the studio," she replied. "My friend became frightened after this, because it was the second time in her life that she had seen a deceased person," Paulina says.

Another time, a guest from Australia couldn't sleep all night, because an old man was talking to her. He told her things she couldn't possibly have known about previously. One of the things he revealed to her was that he was very sad, and the reason for his sadness was that he had died without resolving an on-going fight he had with his brother. Later on the gardener confirmed that this was true. The brothers had fallen out and hadn't made up before O'Gorman died.

"When I decided to rent out this house for a couple of years to be able to travel, the old gardener became furious," Paulina continues.

"I am very mad," he told me, "but Juan is also very upset with this." I told the gardener "Don Antonio, don't worry, I will come back in two years and the people that are going to rent it are very nice people, and they are going to continue to employ you."

"At that very moment I heard a great crash from inside the house and ran in. On the side of the living room and in front of a window were three big shutters, because my children used to watch TV there. These three shutters were held in place by nine strong bolts attached to the wall. At the same time that the gardener told me that O'Gorman was very angry with me, these nine bolts came loose simultaneously and all of them fell down. When I came in they were lying on the floor and the most beautiful light fell into the room through the window. Then I decided never to put them up again."

"It's the light that is the greatest feature here," she tells me. "But also the water."
"The water?" I ask curious.
"Yes, water is always something that is in great demand in a place that often suffers from droughts. O'Gorman was always saying that we are destroying the earth. This is something that can also be seen in his paintings. So he installed seven big containers for water on the roof and a large cistern in the garage too, so we are never left without water."

Earlier she told me about her great love of nature and how much she abhors pollution and the way that it's destroying the earth. As a biologist it's understandable that she is so aware and in tune with nature and her motto is *'I'm the most content when I connect with nature'*. Now it's seems that it's maybe not a coincidence that she has something so fundamental in common with the former owner of this house. After all that I have heard about him and this house, a home that they both seem to share in harmony, I can only conclude that he must like her very much.

"How would you describe your interior design style?
"I can't say that I have a specific style in my home," she states. "I have never bought a single piece of furniture. Everything I have is inherited. The sofa is from my ex-husband's home. I reupholstered it in this *Trisha Guild* fabric, and it still looks the same after more than 20 years. Most of the furniture I inherited from my mother. I haven't done anything to the house itself so it's intact. The mural in the dining room is O'Gorman's signature piece in the house. I have heard people think that it's a pity to live in a functionalist house and not have matching furniture. But for me a home is a place where I feel comfortable. I'm not a purist. What I do like are objects. I love the ceramic pieces from *Ameca* for example."

"My greatest inspiration is my grandmother who had a historical house here in *San Ángel*. It was huge, about five times bigger than this house. It was a 1700s hacienda and she had an eclectic way of decorating it."

"What I like about my home is its generous size. Last week we had a wedding reception here for our youngest son and there were 150 guests here. Yesterday I held a meeting here for about 15 people. People visit my showroom almost every day when I'm here. But when I'm alone and upstairs it has a more intimate and cosy feeling."

"What I love the most about living here is the energy that this neighbourhood has. The moment I pass the first of its cobbled streets, I feel relaxed. It still feels like the small town that it was, before it became engulfed by the city. When I walk around the neighbourhood with my dog, I always discover something. I passed a Japanese Mandarin tree one day and the fruits were falling off it. I asked the guard if it would be permitted to pick the fruit and he said it would. Then I went home to fetch a basket and brought enough back with me to make marmalade. This kind of thing couldn't happen in the city, even in such a nice area as La Condesa."

"What would your dream home be if you didn't live here?"
"I have had a dream for a very long time and I have finally realized it. I fell in love with a remote place on the *Oaxaca* coast, close to the sea. I love the place because it's very well preserved, not developed at all, and it will always stay like this. After visiting it for many years, I got the opportunity to buy a small piece of land in the forest. Here I have constructed an experimental house made of earth, with the help of a cousin who is an architect. It's a permaculture project, and very simple but it has a vegetable plot where we grow vegetables, which is difficult because the area is very dry. My stepson and his wife live there too and I enjoy being a part of the community. My life is very simple when I'm there. I have all the things I need in one box. The house doesn't have any electricity, only candles, so I go to bed early and I sleep well, like I never have done in any other place before. It's so peaceful and I'm at peace with myself when I'm there."

"What does a home mean to you?"
"A home is a place that has a good energy. It's place where you really can recharge yourself in a positive way, so that you enjoy living in the moment."

— A home is a place that has a good energy. It's a place where you really can recharge yourself in a positive way, so that you enjoy living in the moment.

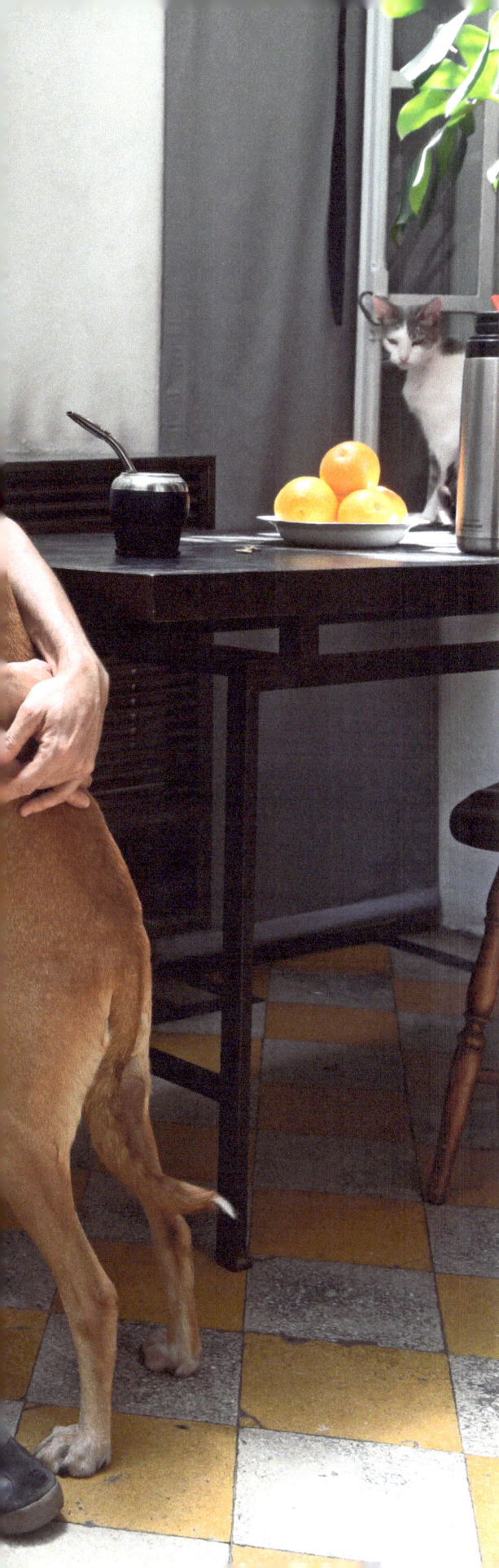

NICOLÁS

PALERMO VIEJO, BUENOS AIRES

Nicolás Cunto
Architect
Business owner

A PEACEFUL HAVEN

PALERMO VIEJO, BUENOS AIRES

I'm in the home of Nicolás Cunto in Buenos Aires. He is an architect and he also owns a business, where he sells bags and accessories of his own design.

As an independent architect, he carefully chooses the projects he engages in using two criteria. Projects that he likes, or projects that involve people that he likes. He undertakes about two a year, mainly because his business takes up most of the working hours.

"Working as an architect I like to work with people who have a dream. And then I can dream with them," he says.

He is currently designing a coffee shop in a museum he loves, called *La Abadia*. He has also designed and built a cutting-edge modern beach house for himself in San Antonio in Uruguay. It's a house with large windows that allow nature to flow in and become a part of it. And the way that it's constructed makes it look like it's floating above ground. He has designed the house in this way, because he doesn't want it to impact too much on the wildlife in the area. The elevated position of the house allows animals to pass underneath it.

His home is in Palermo Viejo, a more quiet and residential area than the livelier Palermo SoHo or Hollywood. It's less developed, as the building regulations stipulate low-rise buildings of no more than twelve meters height. The architectural style of his house is called *PH, Propiedad horizontal*, a variation of the *Casa Choritzo*, typical for Buenos Aires, where the majority of the building plots are long and narrow. The individual units and rooms in these buildings are lined up in a straight row, long and thin as a Chorizo sausage, each reached from a long and narrow, roofless corridor leading from the front door.

These two-storey dwellings are neither apartments nor houses, but something in between, and quite unique for this part of the world. They each have individual patios, providing fresh air and ventilation. The street-side unit of the PH houses has its own exterior door and the two units behind it, have a shared exterior entrance.

The long and narrow passage that leads from the entrance has checkered blue and white tiles on the floor. Nicolás's home is the first one leading off it, behind a tall metal door inset with coloured glass. Beside his front door he has a small herb garden attached to the wall and his bicycle is parked beside it.

Stepping inside his home I'm in a small courtyard that is now a room, since his patio is glazed over with a greenhouse roof. It's a bright space with a fantastic ceiling height. Huge potted plants, a banana tree and a Ficus, are high up on a ledge. The sunlight slants through a grid made of bamboo, giving much needed shade. Two ceiling fans are rotating slowly, circulating the air that comes in from the front door, an open window to the passage and the open door of a roof terrace. Leading off this downstairs patio-room is a small kitchen and a living room. Up one flight of stairs and on a small landing is a bathroom and another flight up is a bedroom and an open roof-terrace that has a large collection of plants.

Nicolás tells me that the PH houses are extremely sought after and that he was very lucky to find one in this area, as it's close enough for him to walk or to ride his bike to work. He likes the character of these houses, often a hundred years old. Knowledgeable about the architecture of Buenos Aires, he explains about the interaction that Argentina and Europe had historically.

Argentina exchanged wool from sheep in Patagonia and meat and grain from the Pampas, for wood and other building materials from Europe. But not only building materials. Even whole palaces were dismantled and shipped over in parts. In his house the wooden pine floor came from France, and other wooden details came from Bolivia, as Argentina didn't have any trees of its own at that time. The trees we see here today are all imported and planted.

He shares his home with his dog Paco and his cat Emma, named after a well-known female Buddhist nun. And indeed, this home has a very peaceful ambience to it. Nicolás, a peaceful man himself, tells me that although not a practising Buddhist, he shares a lot of values that can be described as Buddhist. He often meditates when he's out on long walks around town with his dog. Originally from Italy, his grandparents came to Buenos Aires around the time of the First World War.

"I like to be at home, to cook and to take care of the plants," he tells me. "I enjoy being alone. And I relish silence. There is a famous saying in Italy: *'Il dolce con niente'*. It means *'The sweetness of doing nothing'*. Our culture now is very fast-paced and stressful. It's all about producing, delivering and being efficient. So I like to indulge in the sweetness of doing nothing as often as I can."

"Silence is very important for me and it was an important factor when I was searching for a place here in Buenos Aires", he says. And his home is really

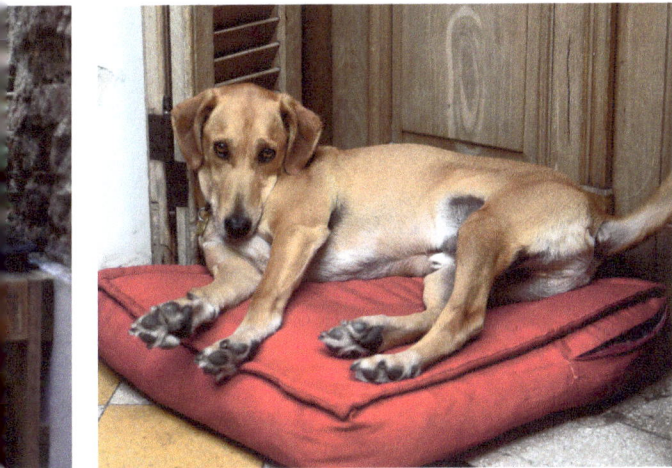

extremely quiet. There isn't a hint of the bustling city outside populated by the 2,9 million inhabitants called Porteños.

"This house is like an island," he continues. "We could be anywhere, in a remote village or in the countryside. But step outside and the city is there with everything a big city can offer. So it's like having the best of two worlds."

"Do you have a motto in life and if so what is it?"
'I search for inner peace.'

"Do you have a favourite place you like to spend time in?"
"In summer it's the living room because it's cool in there. And I like to sit on the roof-terrace at night looking at the moon. The kitchen is also a favourite place because I love to cook. I mostly eat raw food but I also like Mediterranean cuisine very much."

"Do you have a favourite piece of furniture?"
"There is a lamp from Norway that I really like. And the bookshelf in the living room is of my own design, so of course I like it too. I made it from old floorboards I got from an apartment I was renovating. But I must say that I'm not attached to things. I believe that attachment to things make you unhappy. At the end of the day you will lose everything and if you are too attached to things and you lose them you will suffer."

"How would you describe your interior design style?"
"Eclectic. But I enjoy surfaces more than style. The materials things are made of. I love, for example the spirit of the workbench from a carpenter that's in the corner. The weight and the feeling of it. I wouldn't say that I have a specific style, though I used to have mostly contemporary furniture. Now they are in the beach house in Uruguay. That house is very modern and very empty. They fit in there. That house is a container of moments. Here I have inherited furniture from my father. In the living room the sofas are the two beds where my parents slept from the first day they were married. I don't like the style but I like the history of it."

"As people we change," he continues. "This is another Buddhist concept. What we like today we don't like tomorrow. What we liked yesterday we don't like today. So I'm consistent in what I like today."

"Where do you get your inspiration from?"
"When I design I take my inspiration from inside myself. I love colours, preferably strong colours. But I use them sparingly and with thought. The very vivid blue colour on the wall of the rooftop terrace for example came from a desire to see a blue summer sky from my bed all year around. I also like the soft colours from the 50s. Grey is very neutral and I chose it for the bedroom, as it has to be restful. My home has to be a place where I can rest and relax. There is too much information outside. But it doesn't have to be

— *For me the most important things in a home are the living things. Paco, Emma, the plants and me. That energy is what makes it a home.*

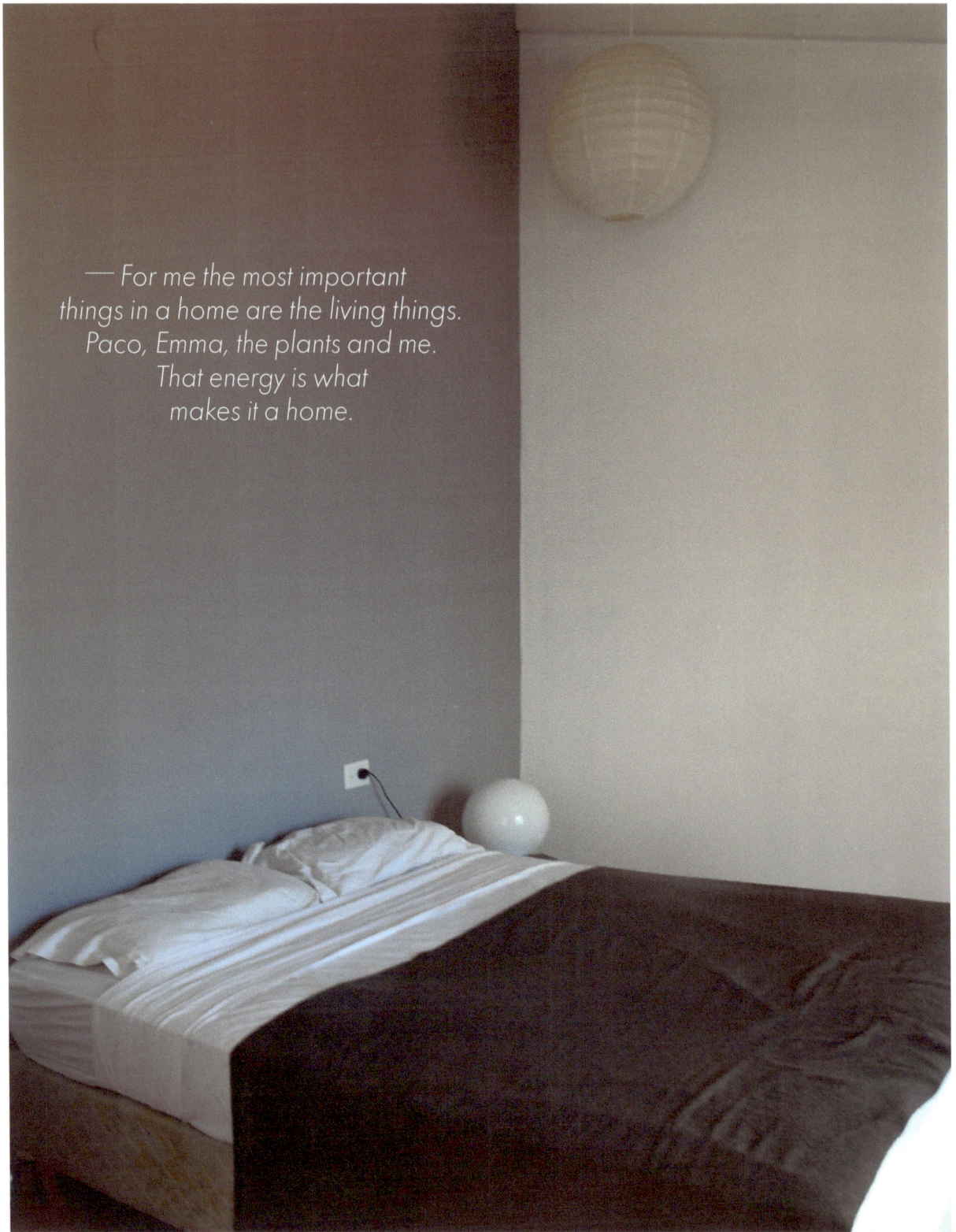

minimal. I need plants. And I need the different areas of the house for what they offer."

"What is the best project that you have carried out here in your home?"
"The bamboo roof of the patio without a doubt. It changed the light and the temperature in here. We wouldn't be able to sit here otherwise."

"What is the best advice you can give people in terms of making a home for themselves?"
"Be yourself. And choose things you like."

"What would your dream home be if you didn't live here?"
"I would love to live by the sea and be surrounded by olive trees. I love to swim in the sea. I love the smell of the sea. It would be in a place where the water is luscious and translucent and the houses are dazzling white and bold blue."
"It sounds a bit like Greece to me," I say.
"Yes perhaps my perfect dream home would ideally be not one but two houses. To have two homes, one in each hemisphere. This way I would always have summer."

"What does a home mean to you?""My home is the most important place on earth. A home is a place that you make into a home," he emphasizes.
"For me the most important things in the home are the living things. Paco, Emma, the plants and me. That energy is what makes it a home. The most important thing of the home is the energy that you generate inside it. The rest is a container."

FRANKLIN & JOHN

MANHATTAN, NEW YORK

Franklin Vagnone
CEO
Cultural consultant and lecturer
Author
Architect
Sculptor and painter

John Yeagley
Director of project management,
education and reseach

THE COLLECTORS' PARADISE
MANHATTAN, NEW YORK

I'm on my way to Upper East Manhattan to the home of Franklin and Johnny but first I'm meeting Johnny. He is something of a polyglot and speaks French, Spanish and Russian fluently, with a little Dutch and Turkish thrown in, and is currently studying Arabic. I discover he even has a little Swedish up his sleeve, as he texts me *'Jag är nästan där'*, I'm almost there, just before we meet up at a cafe around the corner from their apartment. A cafe with the appropriate name of Fika, a Swedish word and phenomenon, meaning coffee break, preferably accompanied by buns or cakes. He is going to guide me to their apartment, snugly tucked away beside a church and quite hard to find.

I have seen photos of their home and can't wait to see it in real life, and I'm excited to meet the people who created it.

Franklin is at home and as soon as I get through the door they show me around. For an apartment in New York it's pretty spacious, around 1000 square feet*, and consists of three rooms and a kitchen. But it has only one narrow window at the far end of the living room. However, every room is flooded with daylight via skylights in the ceiling. And every single room is filled to the brim with artwork, antiques, sculptures, paintings, artefacts, books and knick-knacks, tastefully arranged and grouped. The oasis these two collectors have created has a wonderful ambience and I'm eager to begin exploring it.

The arrangement of the rooms intrigues me. Two of them serve as bedrooms and the third as both a living room and their bedroom. There is also a dedicated office space for Johnny in one corner. The small kitchen, where they both cook and eat also serves as Franklin's office.

Over a generous lunch in the kitchen, they explain the layout of the apartment. Franklin has three grown-up daughters; Claire, Emma and Sophie and an ex-wife, Laura. They were married for 30 years, but came to a parting of the ways nine years ago, all very amicable. All three of them are now good friends and go off on holidays together with the girls. Franklin and Johnny need multiple bedrooms as out-of-town family members often come to visit them. Yogi the dog completes the family picture.

equivalent to 93 square metres

"Partnership is about parenting for all three of us. We are a good family, Laura, Johnny and myself. A modern family," Franklin says with a laugh.

"If you had a motto, what would it be?"
"There is one single word that truly sums up what I've always been, and that's diversified," Franklin says. "I never wanted to get a degree in just one thing, or only do one kind of job. I've never wanted to be narrowed down. So my motto would be *Diversify*'."
Turning to Johnny he says: "And you are all about experiencing things". Johnny agrees and says it's the same for him too.
"I've always loved novelty. So my motto would be *Variety*," he says.
"What's the difference between your mottoes?" I ask them.
"They're fairly close," they laughingly agree, and say that's probably why they get on so well together. "We are constantly looking outwards and trying to be inclusive rather than limiting."

We try to tease out the differences between the mottoes they have chosen. "Johnny will walk through the city and purposely not go down the same street twice. If he's going to a place, he'll take a different route every time," says Franklin. "This drives me nuts. I just want to go from point A to point B."
"Sometimes I'll introduce him to something new," Johnny interjects. "It might be an App, some software, a place or a book. And he will get into it, but by then I'll have already lost interest and gotten into something else. Meanwhile he's delved a little deeper."
"Maybe that's the difference between us. I'm very strategic," says Franklin. "Perhaps I have more of a long-term way of looking at things. But there's a lot of overlap between us and that works for us."

The words fly quickly between them. When one stops speaking the other takes over immediately. Sometimes they even say the same thing simultaneously. They are clearly very much in tune.

They go on to describe how they work together. Franklin attends a lot of conferences where he lectures on historic houses. Johnny always accompanies him on these business trips, and he is the one who investigates and researches every locality they visit. He will come up with all kinds of interesting things for them to do, and places for them to explore. The more quirky, unusual and unique these are, the better. Maybe a visit to a small museum exhibiting a meteor that once fell on somebody's head. Or perhaps an impromptu encounter with the local inhabitants. This may result in them gaining a better understanding of wherever they may be, but more importantly, it gives them an intimate feel of the place. This arrangement works well for both of them and they have a lot of fun. I can see how 'diversity' and 'variety' work for them and how well they complement each other.

Yorkville is the least affluent neighbourhood in the Upper East Side of

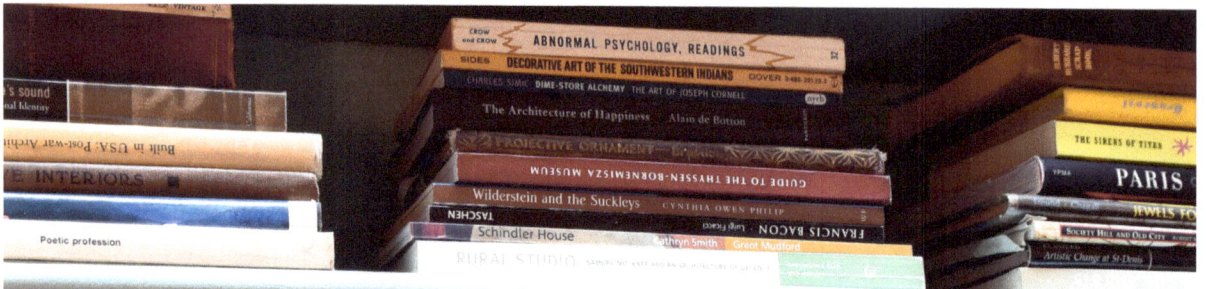

Manhattan and still retains an old German and East European flavour, with lots of restaurants and unique shops. It was the location, in the middle of Manhattan that initially drew them to the area. The apartment was close to what then was Franklin's workplace, and he could easily walk back and forth to work each day. It was also within walking distance of most of the art museums and cultural hotspots that these two cultural fanatics, as they call themselves, crave. It supports and nourishes their lifestyle.

The light is the most important feature, they agree. "Some days, especially in the summertime, it is so bright indoors that you almost have to wear sunglasses," Johnny tells me. "We lived in a apartment before this one that had a lot of windows, but it was considerably darker. The light here is amazing".

"It was a great opportunity," Franklin says. "This space was crying out for a remake and as a designer I saw the possibilities it had for us."

"Coming into the apartment via a private alleyway is way cool," Johnny tells me. "It feels very 'sketchy', very much like New York itself. We cleared the alleyway and filled it with plants and Franklin put up the Italian cafe lights. Now, especially in the evenings when the lights are lit, many people stop to take photos." They marvel at the fact that one of Franklin's daughters found an image of the alleyway that someone had posted on Instagram and that had gone all around the world.

They have lived here for four years now. Before moving in they refurbished the whole place. Sanded the wooden floors and painted them black, using the same colour for the panelling and the mouldings around the doors, and painted all the walls white. They laid bare the transoms above the doors that had been completely hidden and put in the missing glass, making the hallway brighter. And they did all the work themselves.

"How would I describe my interior design style? Well, I'm not driven by any particular style," Franklin says thoughtfully. "I like anything as long as it's good design. And it's not the cost. Because it doesn't really matter to me if something is cheap or expensive. You could sum up my style in one word. Compositional. The reason I put objects together is because of the composition. And this is constantly changing because I will get hold of something new and I will have to redo everything and make a new arrangement."

This home is in flux – constantly evolving and changing. New objects are brought in to replace those that were there before, and the compositions shifts. Old heirlooms are mixed with thrift store finds. Nothing is sacred. As long as it pleases, it works.

"This approach feeds directly into the work I do at house museums," Franklin observes. "Because I argue that house museums should be treated like this. They shouldn't stay the same for years and years on end as if they were pre-

FRANKLIN

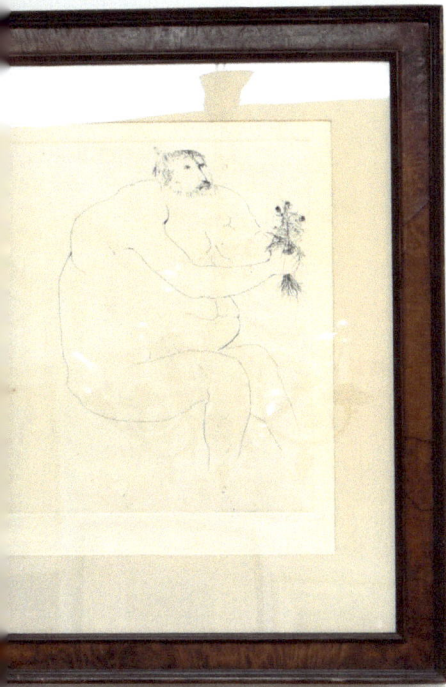

— *Home is a space
that refects who we are.*

JOHNNY

—A home is like a living organism.
You want to take care of it
and infuse it with life. You want to
make that place happy, so that
it makes you happy!

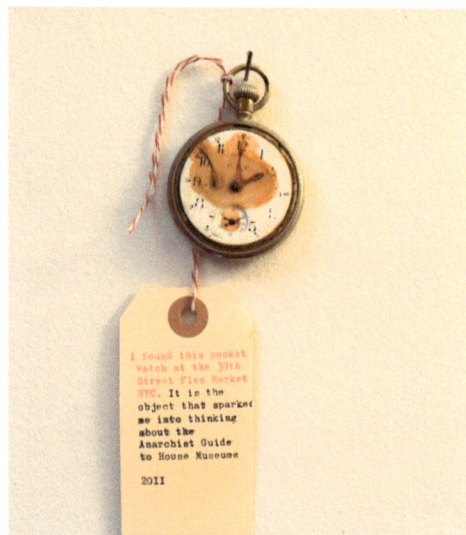

I found this pocket
watch at the 39th
Street Flea Market
NYC. It is the
object that sparked
me into thinking
about the
Anarchist Guide
to House Museums

2011

served in amber. This is what my book is all about. Making historic museums come alive and relevant for people today."

"What is your favourite spot? Where do you spend most time?"
"For me it's my office that's right by the only window," Johnny says.
"He loves that window," Franklin interjects. "In the summertime he opens it up, and the ivy growing outside wafts around in the breeze."
"The alleyway feels like it's our own space, because it's always empty," Johnny says. "It's like it's our garden."
"I pretty much spend most of my day right here," says Franklin, indicating the kitchen where he has his office space. "I love to surround myself with all these things. I keep hanging different things up to look at and I'm constantly rearranging my collectables. But I also enjoy relaxing in the sitting room."
"He has this thing about rearranging things that feeds his soul. I believe it's healthy for us to move things around. It brings different objects to life," says Johnny.
"I agree," Franklin answers. "But I will say this. I feel very happy when I'm giving stuff away. I give things away all the time, to friends and to my daughters. I decided when I turned 50 to start giving stuff away, rather than, when I die, the family being forced to throw all my things that Johnny doesn't want into a dumpster. I want them to take stuff now. I can always find new things in a thrift store if I want."
As an interior designer myself this rings a bell. "Is this just an excuse because what you really want is to go out and get more things?" I ask.
"That might be very true," he says and we all laugh.

We talk about their favourite pieces of furniture and discover that they have quite different tastes. According to Johnny, Franklin values design over comfort, while he himself wants furniture to be comfortable and functional. They joke about Johnny's office chair that is bog standard. In contrast Franklin's is an Arts and Crafts armchair. When it comes to choosing a favourite piece of furniture Franklin has a hard time picking out just one item. There are so many things he loves and feels an attachment to. Finally he decides on the Arts and Crafts rocking chair in the kitchen, which was the first thing he bought together with Laura when they were dating. He also chooses a mirrored vanity piece, which is newly acquired. It is difficult for Johnny to pick out anything in particular, and – here I am guessing – he can't allow himself to become too attached to anything in this shifting environment, where things disappear or appear on a whim. But he loves trays and his favourite is a vintage one, which he brings out to show me. A friend, who is a curator of decorative arts, has pointed out that parts of the decoration were made of butterfly wings.

"Where do you get your inspiration from?" I ask.
"I get my inspiration from things like cityscapes," Franklin says. "I look upon

CASSELL
NEW
GERMAN
DICTIONARY

GIVING **PRESERVATION**

WHAT MAKES A GREAT...

T'S GUIDE TO HISTORIC HOUSE MUSEUMS

things compositionally. I observe the different shapes. Did you see the silver ornaments on top of the bookcase? I see them as if they were church steeples. I get inspiration from things like that. Or from this vintage post-card that Johnny bought in a wonderful thrift shop we had just around the corner, called the 'The Mystery Shack'. Look at the architecture. The shapes I see here inspire me to go and make a setting for a composition. That's how my mind works."

"What is the best advice you can give people about making a home for themselves?"
"I often come into peoples homes and realise that everything's store-bought," says Franklin. "They could have spent half as much money collecting things from their family that are probably up in boxes in the attic and produce an interior that is meaningful to their lives. But for some reason they don't feel safe doing that. By this I mean Johnny and I are secure in who we are. We feel safe to express ourselves, in our home as well as in our lives. My advice would be that you have to find that safe place within yourself. There should be a correspondence between your inner and your outer world. If you find that, your home will naturally evolve out of it."
"My advice would be; don't be afraid of making changes. In fact change is necessary," says Johnny.

"What would your dream home be if you didn't live here?"
Johnny's dream home is a bungalow-style house with a wrap-around porch and a fireplace with a parcel of land around it. It would definitely have a rustic feel to it. Franklin says that for him, he's already had three large southern houses with porches, so he has already done that. But it would be wonderful to move to a plot with two houses sitting on it, in a rural setting surrounded by woodland. A house for Laura and another one for them.
"For me a home is more a connection to people," Franklin says. "Give me a garage and I could make it really cool. But I think that it would be nice for the girls. For them to come home and have everybody there in one place."
But they both agree, that whatever house they will move to in the future it will be a small house.

"What does a home mean to you?"
"One of the reasons why Johnny and I are constantly collecting these things and hanging them up is because our interests continually change and grow. So all of this," says Franklin and waves his arms, "just documents where our minds are right now. So I would say: 'Home is a space that reflects who we are'.
"It's like a living organism. You want to take care of it and infuse it with life. You want to make that place happy so that it makes you happy!" says Johnny.

CECILIA

PALERMO HOLLYWOOD,
BUENOS AIRES

Cecilia Miranda
Business owner
Photographer
Designer
Art Director

VISUAL QUIETNESS

PALERMO HOLLYWOOD, BUENOS AIRES

Cecilia Miranda expresses herself in a multitude of ways. She is a food and lifestyle photographer, a designer, an art director and a business owner. The store she owns is a home accessory shop specializing in cookware in Buenos Aires. Her energy is limitless and she always seems to have something creative going on, while giving a gentle and mild-mannered impression. "Being creative is very fulfilling. I am very happy and satisfied in my life," she says.

She clearly follows her motto, which is: *'Always listen and be true to yourself.'*

Her home is in the leafy area of Palermo Hollywood. It's a spacious three-bedroom apartment of about 200 square metres* with two large terraces, and she shares it with her two daughters, Mercedes and Manuela. They have lived here for two years now and have recently renovated it. The apartment is freshly painted and there is nothing yet on the walls. The door out to the patio is open and the light is flowing in. The old furniture contrasts well with the modern lines and the apartment feels serene. Her daughters' rooms both face the street, but Cecilia's bedroom is a separate small house across the patio. One flight of stairs above the apartment is the spacious rooftop terrace that's embedded in the greenery of the trees that border the street below. Here are tables and armchairs where you can enjoy the summer evenings.

She likes to spend time in the kitchen since she enjoys cooking, and it has a gas hob placed in the centre of one wall. The large dining table and the assorted chairs around it are all old and pieces of furniture that she likes a lot. And the low chair in her bedroom that she tells me is made for sewing is a favourite. It looks like a Thornet chair, but was made to be this low in order for the seamstresses to be able to sew the hems of dresses.

"But I live on the sofa when I'm at home," she says. It's here she writes in her journal, reads or listens to music. Even to sleep on sometimes. Like so many of the homes I have visited, there is no TV. The open bookshelf shows books, magazines, pens, pencils and notebooks that indicate alternative ways to relax. She loves the tactile sensation of things. The rough surface of a tabletop. The nice textile covers and exquisite paper of the books on the coffee table. This trait or sensibility also translates well into her photography.

*equivalent to 2153 square feet

She captures the feeling of textures into her images so well that you can experience the smoothness of a fabric or savour the taste of a crumbling cake just by looking at the photos.

"I'm a visual person and I need to feel things," she says. "But I want them to be aesthetically pleasing too. Even when I was a small girl and everybody sat down at the table and started eating, I wouldn't start to eat before I had composed my food so that it was beautiful on my plate."

"My style is pared down and simple," she continues. "I have few things, but everything I have I either love or they mean something to me. The only thing I change are the textiles depending on the season. In spring and summer I use lighter colours. The greatest feature here is the light. I like that the apartment is very bright."

"My father was a very special man. He has definitely inspired me. People called him *'Negro Miranda'* because he was very dark-skinned and had brown eyes whilst his brother was the opposite; very fair with blue eyes. But he was truly creative, a bohemian and an artist at life you can say," she tells me and shows me a photo of him that was taken in the 60s. In it I see a very handsome man in the company of a woman who was close to him.

"Would you say that your home reflects who you are?" I ask.
"Yes I believe it does. But my store does that too and they are quite the opposite of each other. The store is very busy, chaotic and stimulating in many ways. It's where I create and where I have my photo shoots. And my home is very quiet. Here I need the visual calmness it offers. Both of them have the contrasts that I crave, chaos and calmness."

"What is the best advice you can give people in terms of making a home for themselves?"
"Don't start decorating or renovating a new home at once. Live in it for a while. Have only the bare necessities first and then acquire a feeling for what you need to add. Get to know it. See how the light falls in, how it feels in different seasons and how the space works for you."

"What would your dream home be if you didn't live here?"
"My dream home would be an old farmhouse next to the beach probably in Uruguay, because the climate is so nice there by the sea. It would have a large barn with lots of natural light that I could turn into a workshop and use as a photo studio. It would also have a large kitchen where I could cook and a kitchen garden too, where I could grow my own vegetables. Next to the barn would be a separate house, which would be my living quarters. I see this house as quite small, but big enough for my family when they come to visit."

"What does a home mean to you?"
"A home is a personal space where I do ordinary day-to-day tasks, like cooking and watering plants. Tasks that make me relax and connect with myself. It's a place where I nurture my soul."

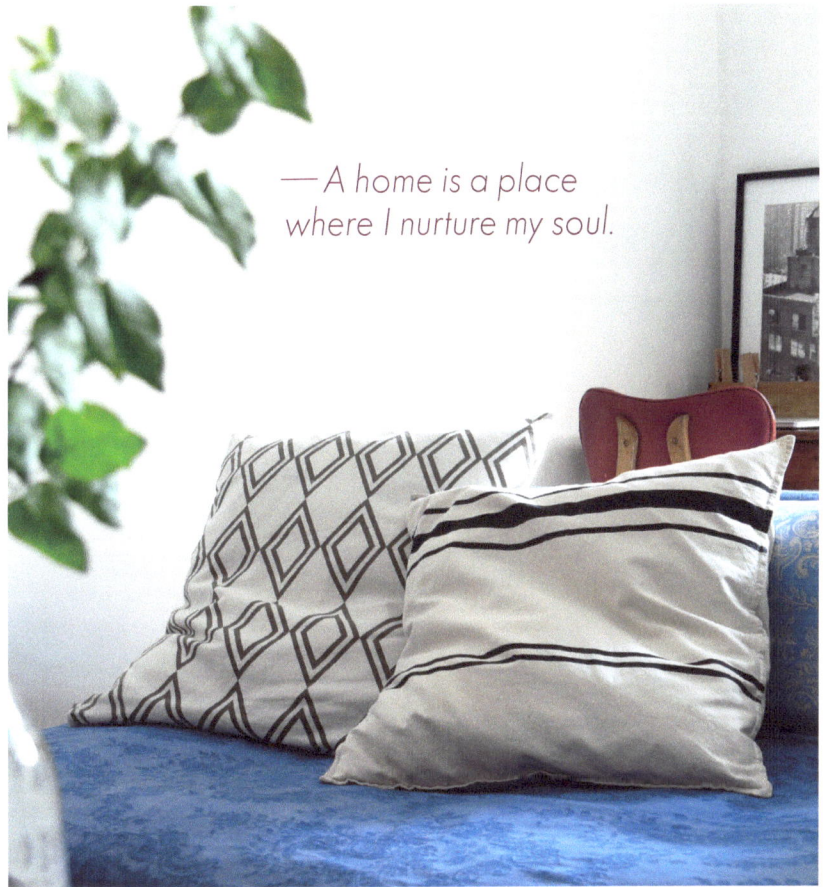

—A home is a place where I nurture my soul.

JONAS

WU WEI CREATIVE PARK, SHANGHAI

Jonas Merian
Furniture designer and maker

Nina Chen
Photographer

INDUSTRIAL LIVING

WU WEI CREATIVE PARK, SHANGHAI

I'm in what was once an old warehouse in an industrial park in the northern district of Yangpu, a good distance from central Shanghai. This is the home of Jonas, his wife Nina and their daughter Anna. It is also here that Jonas has his showroom and workshop, Nina has her photo studio and where both of them have their office. It's obvious that creativity is central in this home. The industrial building in itself and the showroom that takes up most of the ground floor reinforces the feeling of it being more of a workplace than a home. But outside the entrance a collection of potted plants creates a homely feel in an otherwise industrial environment. The names Jonas + Nina + Anna painted on the huge rusty metal door, which is their front door, indicates that this is a home too.

Entering their home I'm initially struck by the vastness of the space and then by the huge variety of objects placed around the large room, all of them made by Jonas. Directly inside the front door are colourful vintage biscuit boxes stacked against the wall, waiting to be turned into lamps. There is a kitchen area in one of the corners of the large room. Over the massive dining table, the light from three ceiling lamps made of kettles gives a cosy feeling. To the right of it is an old door leading into a bathroom and to the left is a door made of reclaimed wood that leads to a bedroom. Behind floor-to-ceiling drapes is Nina's photo studio. Next to it, behind metal doors, is where Jonas has his workshop. The building was originally a single large room open to the roof. Jonas and Nina added a loft, where they have their living room as well as a bedroom for themselves and their daughter. This gives them the privacy of a home but they have an office space up here as well.

When baby Anna arrived they had to take steps to make the place more child-friendly and safe. They enclosed the loft with glass and brick, added a handrail to the staircase and installed air-conditioning to cool and warm their home.

However, only days before I visit, the family moved to the other side of Shanghai, because they unexpectedly received a much sought after place in a kindergarten for Anna. So unfortunately I don't have the opportunity to meet Nina and Anna. But Jonas is here to tell me about the five years that they have been here in the government-owned Wu Wei Creative Park.

"What made you decide to live here?"

"We were tired of being employed so we both quit our jobs," Jonas says. "I wanted to be more creative and Nina wanted to set up her own business as a freelance photographer, so we searched for a place where we could realize this. I'm from Switzerland and my background is in prosthetics and orthotics. Through my education and experience as a prosthetist, I have learnt to work with a wide variety of different materials such as wood, metal, plastics, carbon, silicone, textiles and leather. I have always liked to work with my hands. And I have also become passionate about the upcycling movement. So I needed a workshop to make my upcycled design objects and Nina needed a photo studio. "

When they found this place it was dilapidated and required a lot of work to turn it into what it is today. But they saw that this place would be ideal to both work and live in. However, it was necessary to get in help to do the extensive renovation work. They brought out the buildings original brickwork and repainted the interior of the large 300 square metres* building.

"What is the most important feature?"

"The open space and the light. The ceiling height is nearly six meters and this makes this place so special."

equivalent to 3230 square feet

"Where is your favourite area, where you spend most time?"
"When I don't work it would be at the dining table. It's where we usually end up spending most of our time when we have friends over," he says.

He's referring to the solid wooden table in the kitchen area that he made himself from reclaimed wood from the old town of Shanghai. It's incredibly heavy but by putting casters on it, it moves relatively easily. The table was one of the first things he made when they moved in and sparked his interest for making upcycled objects.

"Where do you get your inspiration from?"
"I get inspiration from the materials themselves. It can be anything from old biscuit tins, tyres, kettles or reclaimed wood. I like big things so I tend to go for that when I design and produce. But it's harder to sell large pieces so I make smaller items like the lamps too."

His biscuit box lamps with touch sensitive lamp control are an interesting combination of Chinese vintage meets Swiss technology.

"How would you describe your interior design style?"
"Upcycled based on mixed and matched vintage and shabby chic."

Jonas has created many of their furnishings. Besides the dining table he has made bar stools from steel and old car tyres and a bookshelf of reused wood and Chinese biscuit boxes. The washbasin in the bathroom he made from an old Chinese style dresser with an integrated porcelain sink. Even the stove he made himself with an old Chinese style table as a base, adding a stainless steel table surface, wheels and a gas hob with a gas bottle hanging system.

"Do you have any favourite piece of furniture or accessories?"
"No not really. I always tend to like my latest project the best. Right now it's the big fan that I made for a Danish company who designs and produces all kinds of fabric. The textile material in the fan is their fabric."

"What is the best advice you can give people in terms of making a home for themselves?"
"Let it happen and don't plan too much in advance. To create something is a process that evolves over time."

"What would your dream home be if you didn't live here?"
"It would be similar to this, but ideally beside a beach. Perhaps in Taiwan because there is everything there; forests, mountains and beaches. It's really a beautiful place and I wouldn't mind living there. We have just moved to the other side of Shanghai, because we received a place at an international kindergarten that we were really keen to have, but we will still continue to use this as our work place for as long as we can."

"What does a home mean to you?"
"A home is a place where I feel comfortable and can be myself."

— A home is where I feel comfortable and can be myself.

ROSARIO & MARTIN

PUNTA DEL DIABLO, URUGUAY

Rosario Gabino & Martin Lur
Business owners
Journalists

LIVING OFF-THE-GRID

PUNTA DEL DIABLO, URUGUAY

Far north on the coast of Uruguay and just forty kilometres from the Brazilian border is the small town of Punta del Diablo. It was formerly a fishing village that has become increasingly popular with surfers, who flock to the beaches Playa de Rivero and Playa de la Viuda. But it's at the quieter end by Playa Grande, which separates Punta del Diablo from Santa Teresa national park, where Rosi and Martin have built themselves an off-the-grid house called *'Vía Verde'.* They live here with their son Telmo and a dog called Trotsky that has adopted them.

Vía Verde, the green way, is a house designed to make the least impact on nature. 150 square meters* split on several levels and with large terraced areas it stands alone on the brink of the sea on the outskirts of the small town. The main house is on three levels and contains the communal area with a small kitchen, five bedrooms and a couple of bathrooms and toilets. It's sparsely furnished with only the bare necessities and with few decorations. At the rear of the house is a separate building consisting of one room, which is Rosi and Martin's private living space.

The location is stunningly beautiful. Just a short walk down the dirt road is the natural beach of Playa Grande, where whales can be spotted, and a bike ride away is the national park. At night the stars are bright and clear and cover the sky like diamonds.

The house is built using both certified woods and local wood from the adjacent national park. It's a *'passive house',* which is a standard for energy efficiency that reduces its ecological footprint. It's constructed to require a minimum of energy to heat it or to cool it. The façade that faces the worst winds that usually come from the southeast, has no windows. The windows and doors of the house are positioned to allow the air to circulate in the best possible way, creating a natural air conditioning. The electricity comes from solar panels on the roof and the water comes from a well on the grounds. There is a wetland pool that filters the graywater and the blackwater goes into a separate tank. A compost takes care of the organic food waste. Everything that is transported here comes either on foot or by bike. There is no washing machine. Instead Rosi washes the bed linen, towels and clothes in

equivalent to 1615 square feet

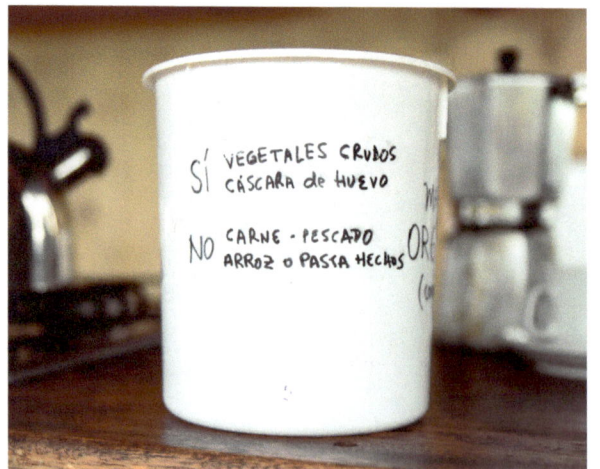

SÍ VEGETALES CRUDOS
CÁSCARA de HUEVO

NO CARNE · PESCADO
ARROZ o PASSA HECHOS

a sink. I'm taken aback by this, but she just laughs and says that it helps her to keep fit.

"You told me earlier that you both had good jobs in London, working as journalists. How come you decided to leave that and come to Uruguay to build yourselves an off-the-grid house?" I ask Martin. It's late afternoon and we are sitting on one of the terraces in the shade of the house. He is taking care of their son Telmo, while Rosi is busy elsewhere.

"I was born in a small town and I lived there till I was 18," he says. After that I studied in Madrid, Paris, London, Geneva, Barcelona and ended up in Buenos Aires. I was in love with big cities and to live in one was my main goal in life then. But then I met Rosi in Buenos Aires and fell in love with her. Both of us come from towns on the 39th latitude, but on opposite hemispheres. And both of us come from towns on the coast. I come from a small town close to the French border in northern Spain. And Rosi comes from a town on the Argentinian coast. We were both working in Buenos Aires when Rosi got a job offer at the BBC in London we thought was too good an opportunity to miss so we moved there. But we were both very clear from the start that we didn't want to stay in a big city like London forever. To find ourselves one day with a baby, looking for a house and a mortgage, thinking about a pension scheme and about buying an apartment on the Costa Brava when we are 60, which is the normal way of life for professionals in Europe. We wanted to come back to South America and start a family in a natural environment. To create a sustainable project and be able to be together as a family on a daily basis."

Before they left for London they did some research on areas that could suit them. Punta del Diablo fitted the bill as a small town by the seaside and when an agent showed them this plot on the outskirts, they fell in love with it. It has wonderful views and is in close proximity to the sea. The project was made possible by Martin's grandmother, who at that time had sold her house at the age of 95 and was able give them the economic basis they needed.

"Has it turned out as you envisioned it?"
"I went into this project with confidence. Even though I had no previous experience of building houses, my father is an architect and both my grandmother and my parents have built their own homes, so I have been able to follow houses in the progress of being built previously," Martin explains. "On the whole it has been a massive learning curve. It's been everything from pleasant, to intense, to exceedingly difficult. When you have an idea in your mind, the reality is always going to be different. But all in all we are pleased with the end result and with the lifestyle it has allowed us to have."

"In hindsight, is there anything you could have done differently?"
"Everything could have been done differently and everything can be improved.

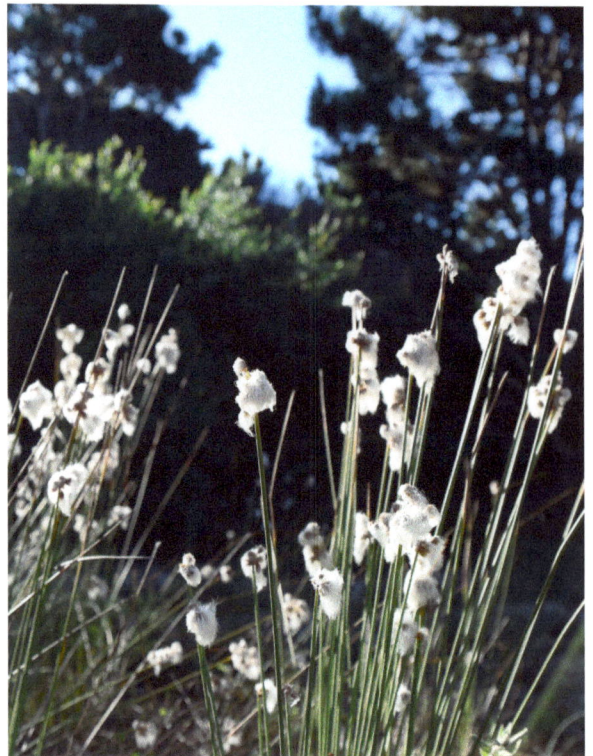

I've had many lessons learned about the implications of building in a remote place like this and of working with different kinds of tradesmen. I've become aware of the importance of working with people who have the right expertise. And I have learned about myself as well. When everything becomes overwhelming and you are out of your comfort zone, you suffer. But it has nevertheless been a good experience," he sums up.

"You had an idea to live in a more sustainable way and to live off-the-grid in harmony with nature. But did it also include the idea of community living?"
"We wanted to live in a more sustainable and green way. But try as we might, we are also inconsistent. We can't always accomplish what we strive for. More than anything, we wanted a place that we could share with like-minded people and learn from each other, so we built the house with that in mind."

"Where did you get your inspiration for this house?"
"I had my childhood home as a role model. It was a large house open to everyone. People always came and went, strangers and friends alike. Every weekend the house was always filled with food, music, old friends and new acquaintances. So we designed this house with a communal area, which is its heart, a place where we can all be together. But there are private areas as well, where people can have their own space. I also worked in hotels when I was studying. I liked the idea of being a host and of making life nice for people. Hospitality comes naturally to me and is something I enjoy."

"You have the house full of people now. We are ten guests staying here and you have your own family with a baby. But you don't have a washing machine or a dishwasher. Does the green lifestyle also entail a more difficult way of living per se?"
"I was very close to my grandparents when I grew up. They used to talk about the time when they were young in the early 1900s. They didn't have any electricity or running water indoors and had to go down to the river to wash their clothes. And the waste they produced had to be reused in some way. But they always claimed that life then was good. It was hard but not unbearable. It's the same here I think. I think that to suffer a little is good. Of course I would like to have all the comforts available in the 21st century. But what I don't want to have are the levels of consumption of the 21st century.

At some point we are going to have a washing machine here too, but perhaps one that is powered by a bicycle? Till then we wash by hand and from time to time we send it away to a laundry service. We also only have a small fridge in the kitchen, the only one that is on the premises as a matter of fact. It's partly because we have to be careful not to use too much electricity. But also because I don't believe we need one. We prefer to use fresh food and go to the supermarket every day. And cooked food doesn't spoil so fast. It can last 12-15 hours at room temperature."

"How is it to live here all the year round?"

I think that we are very lucky to be able to live here. Bit by bit we make improvements. There were only three bedrooms at the beginning. We have added on two more and another bathroom. Last year we built our own house. This is our fourth summer here. In the winter when it's windy and cold, we move into the big house and live in the communal area. Friends come and help us from time to time. All in all it has been a good experience. We also have an international community here in Punta del Diablo, with inspirational people who, like us, are committed to their projects. There is a nice Montessori school that was very small when it started thirteen years ago but since then has grown. The fact that there was a Montessori school here was something that was important for us when we chose where to live. We have a good life."

"Where is your personal favourite area in this house? Where do you like to spend time?"

"I like the front terrace very much because of the views. But all the terraces have something nice to offer at different times of the day. The lower one offers shade when it's warm and sunny and it's pleasant then to spend time in one of the hammocks there. We have friends who made the painting on one of the walls down there and another friend decorated a small side table by the deck chairs."

"Do you have a favourite piece of furniture?"

"The dining table is my favourite, because I built it myself with the help of a friend. The other pieces of furniture a local carpenter built from the wood residue from the house construction."

"What advice could you give to others who might want to build themselves a home?"

"My best advice would be to gather as much knowledge as you can before-hand, even though you are not going to build it yourself. Read books on the subject. Get as much information as you can before you start. There is a famous Spanish saying: *'Lo barato sale caro'*. It means cheap things turn out expensive in the end. This house has been much more expensive than we initially thought. Do things once but do it well, I would say. Another thing when building a house is that you will have to have perseverance. In a project like this there will be lows as well as highs. So it's necessary to cultivate stamina. But the most essential thing to do before you begin is to ask yourself: How do I want to live? It's important for you to evaluate this."

"Do you have a motto in life?"

"When I was young I had an auntie that I was very attached to. She was very old and when she died I went to her house. I found a small box there, and when I opened it there was a single piece of paper inside with a message on it. Written in her own hand it said: *Do not be envious of what you do not*

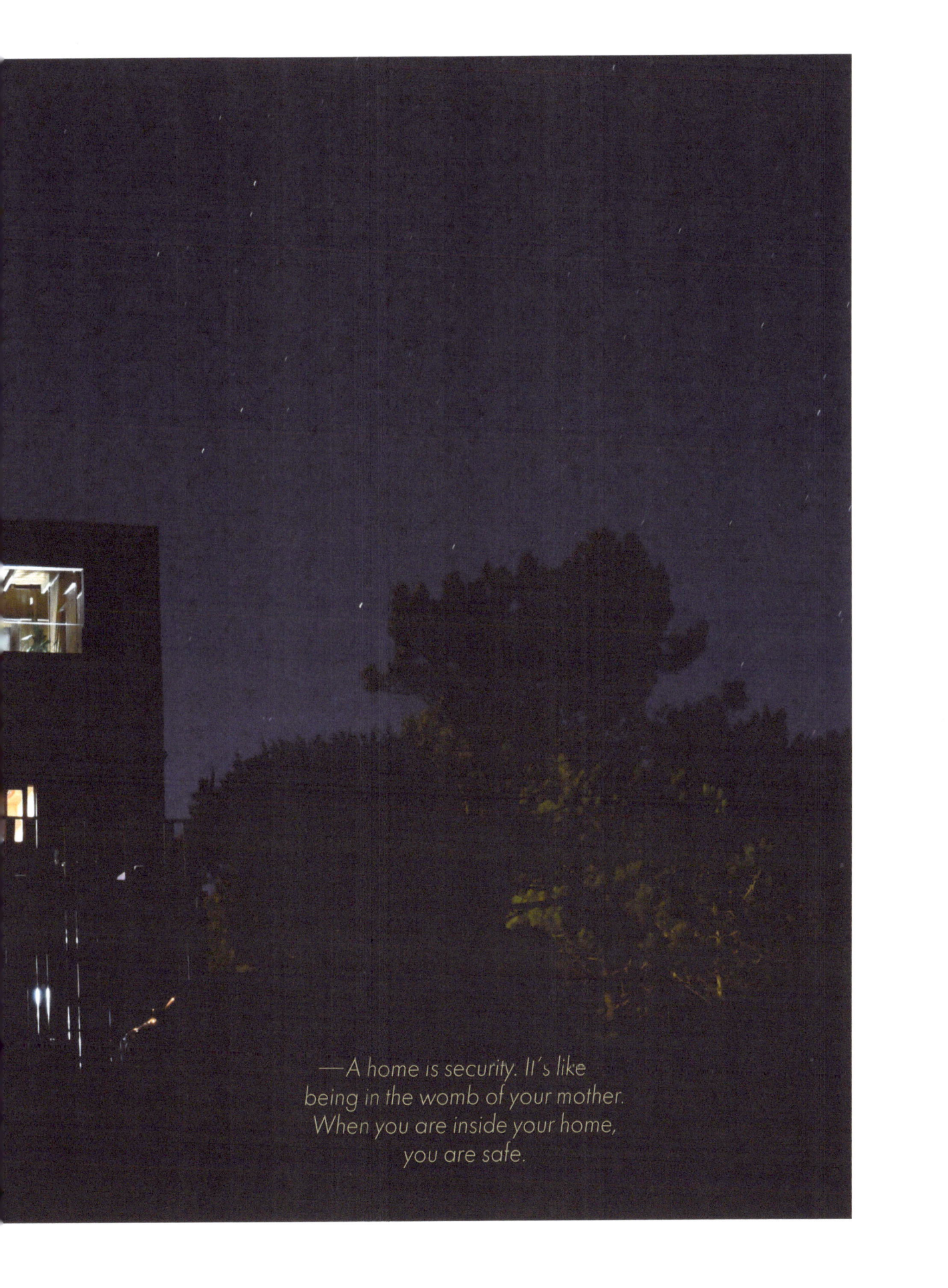

—A home is security. It's like
being in the womb of your mother.
When you are inside your home,
you are safe.

have. But appreciate what you have.' It's a very simple statement but a meaningful one and I have always remembered it.

"One can say that you have already built yourself your dream home and quite recently too. And this is a home where you intend to live for a long time. But if you had a another dream home in mind, what would that be?"
"It would be a house with only one floor situated in the mountains, surrounded by olive trees and fruit trees. It would have views of snow-capped mountains and of woods. It could be in the south of Spain in the Granada area, between the mountains and the sea. We were there on vacation last year as I have family there and it was so beautiful. One day perhaps..."

"What does a home mean to you?"
"A home is security. It's like being in the womb of your mother. When you are inside your home, you are safe."

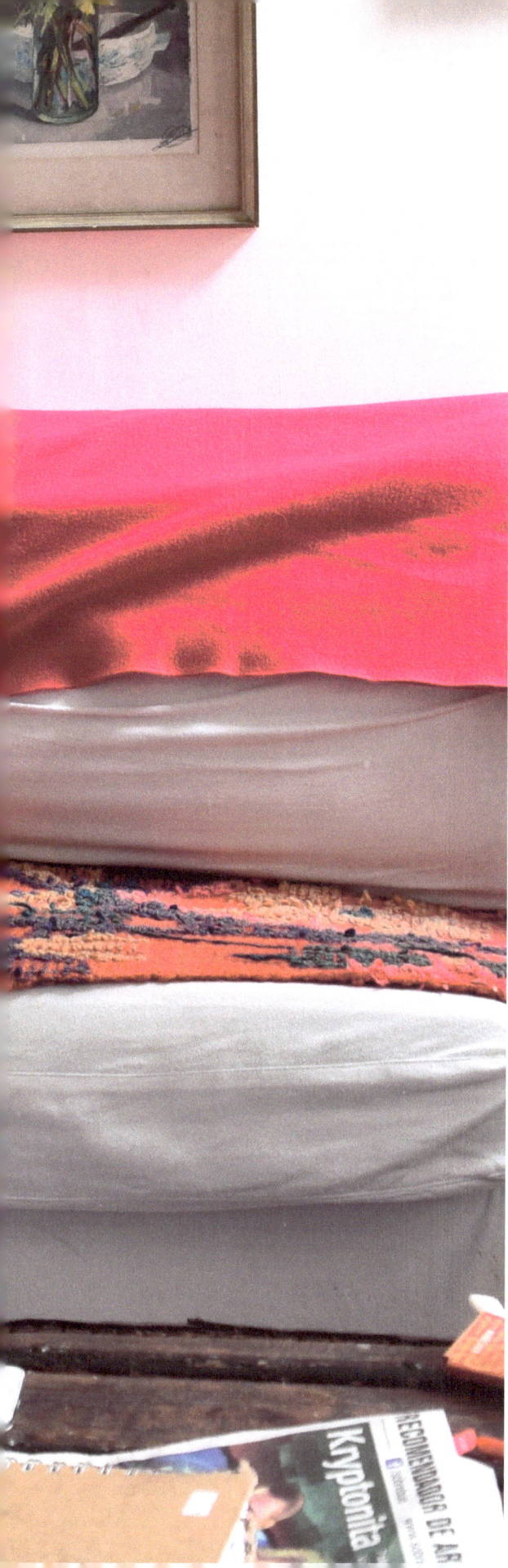

MERCEDES

SAN TELMO, BUENOS AIRES

Mercedes Frassia
Business owner
Architect
Urban Planner

THE HOME OF A TANGO DANCER

SAN TELMO, BUENOS AIRES

Behind a tall door decorated with garlands of flowers on a cobblestone street in San Telmo, Buenos Aires, is the home of Mercedes Frassia. She is an architect and an urban planner, currently running a business in hospitality.

Mercedes's home is in the kind of building that earlier was called a *conventillo**. Behind the tall porch is a narrow passageway that leads out into a yard. Feminine tango shoes sit on top of an old shelf on one wall. This sets the tone for this unusual home. The large house consists of two separate buildings on each side of a garden, which is narrow and deep, sandwiched between two tall house gables completely covered with ivy. In the middle of the garden there is a swimming pool and deckchairs with yellow and white striped cushions. A massive wisteria forms an arch, dividing the yard and adding to the lushness of it. The whole place oozes old world charm. Despite the house being divided into five apartments, they all have the same flamboyant interior design, almost as if they were staged, like a play in a theatre.

"People always said that I was a more of a scenographer than an architect," she confirms.

I enter an apartment in the building at the back through a tall glass door, and come into a large room with an impressive ceiling height of nearly six metres. The whole façade towards the garden is made up of glass windows, which makes it very light. The first thing I notice is a big Goodyear sign high up on one wall. A nod towards the building's brief industrial period perhaps? This detail is a nice contrast to a large chandelier hanging from the ceiling. A massive open fireplace is also prominent.

The apartment has a consistent colour theme with green and red as the two main colours. The green colour is mainly on the windows and doors and on the metal staircase, that leads to the first storey where one of the two bedrooms is found. The red colour is in the decorative elements such as cushion covers, throws and the painted garlands and flowers that adorn the metal kitchen units, furniture, windows and walls.

The sofa is of a modern design. Otherwise, the rest of the furniture is old, some even rustic. But it's the accessories that stand out. Striped tailors dummies, old, oval portraits, an old dresser converted into a washstand, antique

lamp stands, the heavy padded headboard of a bed, demijohns, pictures with tango motifs, old birdcages. This apartment seems to be telling a story.

Mercedes's own home is a small studio on the top level, which is reached though an external stairway. On the small, elevated terrace outside her front door is a Jacuzzi. When I visit, there is a young woman decorating the wall behind it with flower motifs. Her studio has an open-plan kitchen and living room, but the kitchen is mostly unused, as Mercedes claims that she rarely bothers to cook any meals herself, preferring to eat out most days.

She has lived here for thirteen years. When she bought it, the place was run down and dilapidated and everybody, so she says, thought that she was crazy. They believed there was too much work to be done to it. And the barrio San Telmo was very out of fashion at that time. It was a place where the very poor lived. Who would want to live there? But she saw something her architect friends didn't. She saw possibilities.

"That the property had a garden was wonderful. I saw that I could put in a swimming pool," she says. "People in Buenos Aires like to get out of the city and go to the countryside whenever they can, but I'm very urban. To be able to have a large garden in the middle of the city was incredible. And I loved the history of the place. I bought it at once."

The house was built in 1887 and was later turned into a conventillo. After that it became an underground theatre and a bar that became notorious. Then for a short period they printed books in the house at the back. But the rest of the building was empty for years and years. She has renovated it but very lightly, as she has been very keen to keep the character intact.

"I bought this house with a mind to retiring here. But it was too big. I didn't know what to do with it, so I split it into five units. I have lived in all of them myself over time. But now I rent out four of them and live in the fifth. I'm surrounded by people and I love it. I never feel alone. I didn't know that this would be the outcome, so it's been a positive experience," she says.

"One can say that in a sense it has become a conventillo again, but in a different way. In those days the people that lived in a conventillo formed a small community, which I think was good, as I don't believe in the isolated way we live today. It's not a very healthy way of living. Here we have formed a kind of community too. People from different cultures come here to stay, which suits me, because although I'm from Argentina I see myself as being international."

"To take care of the business I needed help. What began as a very small company is now a business with fifteen employees including my son who also works with me. It's good because it means that I can do what I love, which is to dance tango and do my yoga every day."

"You dance tango every day?" I ask.
"Yes I dance every single day. I work till five o'clock. Then I go to my yoga. And after that I go out to dance tango. My whole life evolves around tango. I have been dancing for the past fifteen years. At weekends I dance even more. Then I can dance from 8 o'clock in the evening till 2 o'clock in the morning like a crazy person."

"It must be difficult climbing up those stairs, when you come home with those high-heeled dancing shoes," I remark, seeing in my mind's eye the gaps that are on each of the metal steps on the steep staircase leading up to her studio and the high-heeled dance shoes.

"Ah," she answers. "That's the secret. I dance as a man these days. I have danced for so long, that I prefer to make the choreography myself now. But earlier when I danced as a woman I could dance with anyone. I could dance with a man without teeth and be in love for one dance. To dance tango has very little to do with the other person. It's all about myself. Of what's going on inside of me. I think it's a little bit like meditation."

Her motto is *I do everything my way*' and it becomes evident when she talks about her life. She tells me that she has begun to encourage her workforce to use their intuition at work too. And she has seen the effect this has had, as the staff are much more engaged and involved.

"I never leave San Telmo," she informs me. "Why should I? I have everything I need here within four blocks. There are 50 restaurants. There are orchestra performances every day, so I can dance to live music, and it has all the milongas I could need. I have very few friends left in the other barrios where I used to live. San Telmo is a bohemian place and it suits me perfectly. The only time I leave it is when I go abroad. Whenever I feel stressed I travel, which I love. I have just come back from India, where I attended a friend's wedding."

"Where do you get your inspiration from?"
"I get my inspiration from myself. I never have a plan, only a very general idea of what I want to do, and then it evolves from there. And I never know how long it will take when I start a project. When I find something I like, I repeat that over and over again. Old portraits, trunks, painted things. I like the old Argentinean painted art that is called *Fileteado** and use it everywhere, on doors, windows, walls and on furniture. I love things that are old and I like to make bargains too."

"You have quite a few large portraits on the walls. Can you tell me about them?"
"I found a girl who made these fantastic portraits of famous tango singers. She created them with pastels on paper and they were so wonderful that I couldn't decide which of them I liked the most. So I bought all of them, and have them in the apartments and in the office as well."

—A home is a place where my eyes are happy. When my eyes are happy, my soul is happy.

"Do you have any favourite piece of furniture or accessories?"
"No, though I have inherited some nice old paintings that are quite valuable. The rest is neither very expensive or very special. What I like is the mixture of things and what happens when they all come together."

"What advice would you give to others who want to make a home?"
"The only advice I can give is to just follow your own inspiration. Make it feel enchanting because that will make you happy. I feel like I'm on vacation all the time when I'm here."

"What would your dream home be if you didn't live here?"
"This is it! If I move anywhere I will move around here in the same building, probably to one of the apartments on the ground floor when I can't climb the stairs any more. I wouldn't want to live in any other place."

"What does a home mean to you?"
"It has to look nice because my eyes are very sensitive. I can only be in a place where my eyes are happy. When my eyes are happy, my soul is happy."

* *The conventillos began life as mansions for the wealthy families in Buenos Aires until 1871, when the yellow fever struck the city. This drove away the more affluent residents. The old homes were abandoned or sold at bargain prices. Developers saw the opportunity and snapped them up and rented them to the flow of immigrants that had started to arrive from Europe. These grand former one-family homes in the city centre became tenement houses for the poor, where whole families lived in only one room each, with shared conveniences like bathrooms and kitchen.*

* *Fileteado is a type of artistic, ornamental decoration, with stylised lines and flow-ered, climbing plants, typically used in Buenos Aires. They have been part of the cul-ture of the Porteños, the inhabitants of Buenos Aires, since the beginnings of the 20th century. Many of its inhabitants were European immgrants who brought their cul-ture and traditional art with them. Fused with local traditional art, it has become a distinct style of its own and typical for Buenos Aires and Argentina.*

SAM

SHEUNG WAN, HONG KONG

Sam Chua
Designer & consultant

LIVING BY EAR

SHEUNG WAN, HONG KONG

Sam lives in Hong Kong, in a small studio flat on the 31st floor that has its very own private roof terrace with amazing views over the city.

But we meet in Shanghai, where he's currently on a work assignment. Sam spends much of his time away from Hong Kong for work, but he offers to host me in his apartment when I'm in Hong Kong. I'm happy to accept and look forward to this, as it will give me an opportunity to experience his apartment myself.

We meet at a cafe in the French Concession. Sam tells me a bit about his work as a designer and consultant. When he describes what he does, he uses words like strategy, research, innovation and culture. But mostly, he says, it involves people and problem solving. He spends his days listening to the many layers of his clients. Gathering in-depth information about them and through that knowledge gaining an understanding of what they need.

His motto '*Living by ear*', reflects this well as it parallels the expression 'playing by ear' and it's obvious that he is passionate about his work.

Sam seems to have an in-depth knowledge of himself, as he has a well-defined picture of who he is and what he needs. And it's clear that he has thought a lot about how he wants his home to work for him. He becomes just as passionate when he talks about his home as he was when he was talking about his work. This becomes evident as he describes it. The cafe table between us is soon covered with sketches of the layout and of furniture, which he swiftly draws on a legal pad.

He has had his apartment for about six months and it was the views it had from all three sides and the highly sought after outside space that made him choose it. Even though the apartment is only a modest 323 square feet* it contains everything one can need. A living room with a sofa and a clever sofa table with built in extra seating, a small kitchen, a queen-size bed, a workspace, a bookcase, a keyboard piano, a small desk, storage for clothes and a bathroom.

When I look at photos of the apartment I notice that the colour scheme is very muted, almost monochrome, in soft browns and beiges.

* equivalent to 30 square metres

"Can you elaborate on this?" I ask. "How would you describe your interior design style?"

"Furniture is the frame of life, not the focus," he says. "It shouldn't steal your attention, only support you. So my style could best be described as contemporary and subdued. I'm also pleased how the arrangement of the furniture works as a whole. How I could use what was already there and rearrange it to suit me."

"Where is your favourite area, where you spend most time?"

"I have several areas that I enjoy spending time in. The office space is one of them. Here I can sit and work and have a view from the window at the same time. When I want to unwind after work I read or listen to music and I do that best on the sofa, and I have angled it so I have a nice view from the window on that side as well."

"Where do you get your inspiration from?"

"As a designer I get it from the whole world of course. It's vital for me to look outwards and see the bigger picture at all times."

"Do you think that your home reflects who you are?"

"Yes, definitely. It's less about showing and all about being."

—A home is a place that
helps you be the most 'you'
you can be.

"What is the best advice you can give people in terms of making a home for themselves?"

"I would say understand your needs and your location. Your home should complete your environment. For example my home has plants to create the greenery my immediate environment lacks. You can't copy and paste your home from some other place. So be aware of your needs and don't forget to include your surroundings too," he says with a smile.

"What would your dream home be if you didn't live here?"

"I don't believe in dreams as such. I'm living in a dream home right now you could say. For me, it's about knowing yourself and knowing when to take an opportunity when it arrives."

"What is a home to you?" I ask.

"It's a place that helps you be the most 'you' you can be. My home is my oasis. It makes me refreshed and recharged. Hong Kong is a dense, congested and noisy place. My home helps me to complete my environment, so it's calm, subdued and quiet."

As I had the opportunity to stay in Sam's apartment myself, I can confirm that it is indeed a calm haven in the bustling and busy city, just as he described it. It was very quiet being on the top floor. The calm tones of the interior made the different areas with their various functions come together nicely as one space. And the greenery created with the plants gave a hint of a nature that was beneficial. The space was cleverly designed to make the most of storage areas. The bookcase acted as a room divider, thus creating a bedroom. But the best part was of course the private roof terrace, which I enjoyed immensely. There I felt like I was at the top of my own kingdom.

THANK YOU

I would like to thank the people in this book for welcoming me into their homes and sharing their stories with me. Thank you for your hospitality and generosity. Thank you for responding tirelessly to my endless questions. Thank you for your patience while I photographed your homes. It has been wonderful to get to know each and every one of you! This book wouldn't exist without you.

Thank you Doreen de Waal and family, Erika Krutzfeldt, Eyal Cohen, Emily Johnston, Carin Lilienfeld, Elissa Ehlin, Paulina Parlange Pizarro, Nicolás Cunto, Franklin Vagnone and John Yeagley, Cecilia Miranda, Jonas Merian and Nina Chen, Rosario Gabino and Martin Lur, Mercedes Frassia and last but not least Sam Chua.

I would also like to thank my family for your loving support, encouragement, proofreading and helpful tips. Thank you Calle, Mimmi, Nelly, Paul and Zina.

Lastly thank you both old and new friends for assistance and friendship. Both are needed in the realization of a dream.

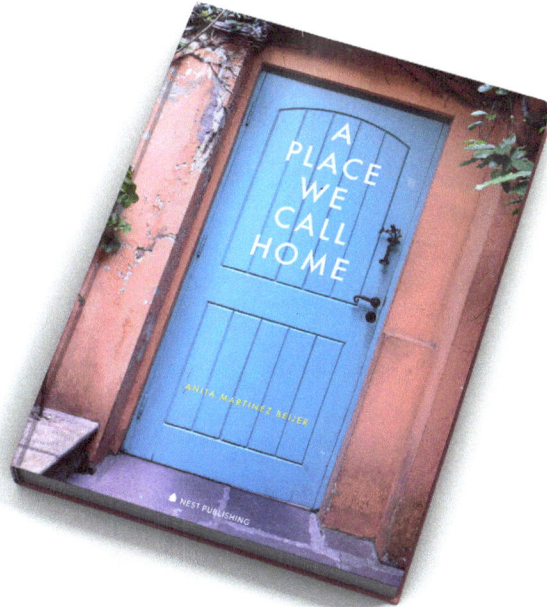

Did you enjoy this book? I would be very happy if you would like to share your thoughts about the book by writing a review and post it at the site where you purchased it. Thank you kindly for your support!

The sequel, *A place we call home,* will be published shortly.
Hardcover ISBN 978-91-984455-2-7
Ebook ISBN 978-91-984455-3-4

ISBN 978-91-984455-0-3

🏠 NEST PUBLISHING

Published by Nest Publishing
info@nestpublishing.com
www.nestpublishing.com